DAUGHTERS OF THE BUFFALO WOMEN

Maintaining the Tribal Faith

Beverly Hungry Wolf

Canadian Caboose Press

Also By Beverly Hungry Wolf:

THE WAYS OF MY GRANDMOTHERS
BUFFALO, BERRIES and HERBS

And with Adolf Hungry Wolf:
SHADOWS OF THE BUFFALO
INDIAN TRIBES OF THE NORTHERN ROCKIES

Copyright 1996
Canadian Caboose Press
Canadian Cataloguing in Publication Data
Hungry Wolf, Beverly, 1950-
Daughters of the buffalo women
ISBN 0-920698-56-5
1. Siksika women--Alberta. 2. Siksika women--Montana. 3. Siksika Indians--
Social life and customs. I. Title
E99.S54H87 1996   971.23'00497   C96-910645-9

Front Cover Painting:
Picunnie Pemmikan Makers, by Winold Reiss.
The woman in the red dress is Cecile Boy, daughter of Bird Rat-
tler and an aunt of the author's mother. She is seen making
pemmican with an old lady named Ragged Woman, the wife of a
warrior and buffalo hunter named Bear Medicine.
The artist first came to the Blackfeet from his home in Germa-
ny during a blizzard in the winter of 1920. Given the name
"Beaver Child," he worked with them for the next 33 years to
paint all the leading tribe members in a series of highly accu-
rate and widely known portraits. This cover scene comes from
the Great Northern Railroad collection through the courtesty
of his son W. Tjark Reiss.

Contents

Foreword

I would dedicate this book to my mother, Ruth Little Bear, except that I already did so with my first volume, *THE WAYS OF MY GRANDMOTHERS*. That time she helped me a lot, but the main stories were from women much older than her, born around the time our people ended their buffalo hunting. Those were the last women able to pass down directly the knowledge and spiritual ways of a tribal life so much different from anything that we know today. I feel honored to have spent time with them and thankful that they let me help with that passing-down process.

Those "Buffalo Women" are now all gone - the last few passed on in the 1980's - though their legacies remain very much alive. Our elders today are the daughters and granddaughters of those Buffalo Women. They lived in an interesting transition period between the buffalo era and our modern times.

As with my earlier volume, these are mostly stories and thoughts from among my own people, the Blood tribe of the Blackfoot Confederacy, living on the Northern Plains next to the Rocky Mountains. There are many more stories like these throughout our continent, waiting yet to be heard. Perhaps the following pages will help encourage the continued survival of native culture and revival of its spirituality, so that some day those who are of my age will also be asked to tell our stories to the next generations. Among them I encourage especially my daughter Star and all my nieces.

Many laughs and warm emotions went with the visits that resulted in these recorded stories. Sometimes we spoke and taped in Blackfoot, other times in English. I have tried to interpret what was said in as meaningful a way as possible. Since Blackfoot was never a written language, those who speak it depend a lot on visual contact to add meaning to their words, though this is hard to convey on paper. In that regard, my husband Adolf again helped me with the lengthy process of sorting piles of notes and transcribed conversations into chapters of readable text. In each case I have read back to these women their stories to obtain final approval.

The first year of work on this project was funded by a grant from the Canada Council; other years were done on my own.

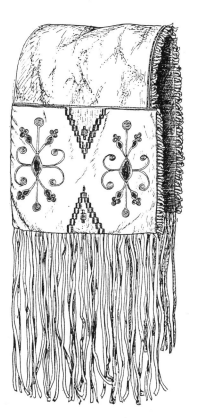

Introduction

It hasn't been much more than one hundred years since my great-grandfathers hunted their last buffalo and my great-grandmothers tanned the hides, using the meat as their main daily food. Members of the Blackfoot Confederacy, to which I belong, had their final great buffalo hunts around 1880, after which they had no choice but to give up their nomadic life and settle down on four designated reservations, three in Alberta and one in Montana.

In their young days, my mother and father heard a lot about that buffalo past from the older people who then still made up much of the tribe. They have often said to me that it was hard imagining such a life, so much different from their own, even though back then it had just ended thirty or forty years earlier. For boys like my dad there was an immense contrast between his fairly uneventful reservation life and the constant tales of war raiding and wild animal hunting of previous generations. It was an especially frustrating time for our men, as they could no longer go out and prove themselves in our traditional ways, through daring deeds and successful hunts. Instead, to get food and other necessities for their families they had to try learning a different kind of life, else they were humbled into relying on government handouts.

For girls of my mother's generation there was much less contrast between the past and current ways of life. Their mothers still did many of the same basic things as back in the buffalo days, such as taking care of their households, bearing and raising children, making meals and clothing for their families.

Their appearance didn't change much compared to the men. Long cotton dresses and moccasins were still common, and most women continued to wear their hair long and braided. Sure, they cooked with beef instead of buffalo, sewed more with cloth than with tanned leather, and relied on stoves instead of open fires. But their one-room cabins were arranged with the beds around the walls, just as in a tipi, only now they could put their kids to sleep at night without worrying what might come to harm them during the darkness.

Sometimes I wonder what might have happened on this continent had our native women been left undisturbed until now to raise their families based on tribal skills and values. Instead, North American society imposed an agenda whereby the Indian people were to be turned into "normal citizens," and this was to be done mainly by taking all Indian children away from their families at an early age and giving them strict indoctrination at various kinds of schools. My mother was among those women in our tribe who experienced the full force of this European style schooling during its first decades on our reservation. It is with profound admiration that I can say she holds no bitter feelings about that time, nor towards its people, though she now regrets having missed out on so much of her own culture and teachings because of it.

The women in this book are in some ways like sisters to each other, the survivors of a fading generation. Too soon they'll be gone, so now is the time for us to hear their stories and try to learn from their experiences. One recurring theme I find while listening to them is that in spite of difficult challenges and seemingly constant poverty, you can be rich in friendships and find plenty to make you happy. They worked hard, prayed often, and helped each other as much as they could. Together they shared our tribal life and kept it going during a most important changing time.

1.

Childhood Days in the 1920's
As recalled by my mother, Ruth Little Bear

"My grandmother's name was First-to-Kill; she was married to White Elk, who was better known as Heavy Head. He was one of the last old-time Blood Indians to go on war raids and to be pierced at one of our Sun Dance ceremonies. My grandmother grew up in the buffalo hunting days, living in a buffalo hide tipi and sleeping with buffalo robes as beds.

"When I was a little girl, around the 1920's, this old grandmother would sometimes gather us kids together and perform a little ceremony. She would paint our faces with sacred earth paint while praying, then she would have us take some of our old, worn-out clothing and she would bring us to a certain big rock on the prairie near our home. There, she'd say to us: 'Leave those things on that rock - give them to the Sun,' and she'd pray for us again. Our things became offerings; that was her way to show gratitude to the Creator, to the Sun, and to other Spirits."

That's one of the special memories my mother has often recalled for me from her childhood. She was awed by that old lady, by her abilities to understand so much about a way of life from the past, a tribal and cultural way that my mother only understood a little. First-to-Kill was giving her grandkids a taste of a life in which it was considered good luck to treat things such as wearing apparel with respect and reverence; instead of just throwing them out, showing thankfulness for the comfort and protection they have given.

First-to-Kill always called my mother by her Indian name

Pretty Crow Woman, and she spoke to her only in Blackfoot. Although she is just three generations away from me, First-to-Kill's life was so different from anything we experience today as to make it almost impossible for us to really understand it. Yet I feel very strongly connected to the spirit of her living, and this has become a major force in my own life.

As I have been watching my mother growing older I realize that she has herself become something like First-to Kill, a fading link to a tribal legacy that combines nature with many kinds of spiritual feelings. My mother's constant faith in prayers and her lifelong interest in natural remedies are among some of the ancient traits passed down by her grandmother First-to-Kill, and later by other medicine people that she was around. These included my dad's grandfather Eagle Plume, who happened to be instructing First-to-Kill's husband Heavy Head in some of his ceremonial knowledge in my mother's younger days. Heavy Head was among the final group of Bloods to fulfill vows made in times of great danger, saying that they would sacrifice themselves in the piercing ceremony. It was then outlawed for nearly 100 years, but has lately been revived.

An interesting aspect of this tribal continuation is that in my mother's youth everyone was convinced our past traditions were dying out. She never imagined to be passing on this old time knowledge to her daughter's family so it could again be used as part of a way of life.

> *"My grandmother was very strict with her traditions and culture. She remained a genuine old-time Blood Indian woman right to her very end, which came in 1949. She tanned and smoked her own hides, wore nothing but moccasins on her feet, along with colourful cotton gowns that we called 'squaw dresses.' Her hair stayed long and dark and she always wore it in braids. She supported her husband Heavy Head, who was a busy and important medicine man in the tribe, while she herself was also frequently called upon to deliver babies and make medicines for ailing people.*

Heavy Head and his wife First-to-Kill, carrying eagle wing fans and dressed to attend the ceremonies they frequently took part in. Heavy Head went on one of the last war raids, in the late 1800's. During great danger he vowed to be pierced at a Sun Dance, thus experiencing an extreme test of faith that was then outlawed by the government for the next 100 years. First-to-Kill was a wise and jovial old lady, known for her healing powers and skilled at the women's part of the ceremonials led by her husband. She was originally married to a German immigrant named Joe Trollinger, with whom she had five children, including my grandmother Pretty Woman (baptized as Hilda Trollinger). Heavy Head was unable to have children, so when he later married First-to-Kill he gladly took her mixed-blood children as his own. Growing up around this old couple's household left strong impressions on their granddaughter Pretty Crow Woman, who is my mom.
Provincial Archives of Alberta Photograph Collection

"Whenever I was still at home I would move to the Sun Dance camps with my grandmother. I can still picture her, the way she loaded up her camping gear and supplies. At that time everything was still done with horses. Sometimes my older brother Howard would be with us, and we'd help the old lady. But she was very strict with the way we acted and behaved, especially around our grandfather, since he was a medicine man; also around his visitors, who were usually respected friends and fellow medicine men. The same went for their women.

"For instance, we couldn't walk in front of these old people while they were smoking. In those days they usually used their pipes, but the same also went for cigarettes. We were told to sit still while they were praying, which was often, and for long times. They also sang sacred songs, a lot of which are lost now.

"My grandmother wouldn't allow us to step over anyone's legs or bodies, out of respect, nor could we eat while laying down. Indoors, we were not allowed to run around and be noisy. That's sure different from the way most kids act nowadays. We couldn't even sit on our grandfather's couch - his bed - which he kept on the floor. He was a proud and holy man; he had spiritual powers. Those were our customs, our ways of showing respect.

"While I was young my grandmother really kept her eyes on me. I was always supposed to sit down on my legs, out of modesty, and I was never allowed to play with boys, especially not to wrestle with them. When I went outside I was only allowed to play with girls who were my age or younger. But sometimes she used to hire an older girl to comb my hair and watch after me, when she got too busy cooking for her and my grandfather's many guests. She was a very responsible woman because she had powers of her own, and this fact helped me early on to realize that such powers are available to anyone, man or woman.

My mother Pretty Crow Woman, wearing a calico dress and cowrie shell necklace, in a haymaking camp somewhere out on the prairies. Sleeping on the ground and cooking over open fires was still part of daily life here, even though the buffalo were gone, so my mom is kind of standing in a timewarp for this photo. The look she's making might describe what will be coming into her life next, moving into a strict boarding school and being forced to learn a much different kind of life.
Collection of Good Medicine Foundation

"In my grandmother's tipi I had my own bed, complete with willow backrests, right at the foot of hers on the south side where the women sit. In the evenings as soon as it started getting dark I was told to come in; I was never allowed to stay outside after dark.

"For toys I had a rag doll and some quilts. Also, we would dress up our puppies and pretend they were babies. I recall my mother getting frustrated with me because I'd keep unwrapping my puppy-baby and then ask her to rewrap it. We used to take things like cardboard

*macaroni boxes and make them into wagons in which
we'd stuff buckbrush and pretend we were hauling home
loads of firewood. Sometimes we'd imagine ourselves in
tipis, other times it was tents, even though we were really
just sitting out in the open.*

*"My grandmother took part in a lot of ceremonies - in
our ways the woman is a full partner with her man. I was
always expected to go to these ceremonies and get my
face painted by whoever was the leader, whether it was
during a Medicine Pipe bundle opening or some other
event like the Horn Society dance. My main job was to
run errands for my grandmother, though sometimes when
they were really busy with ceremonies they would send
me back home for a few days to my parents, not far away
on our farm. My mother and father were usually too busy
farming to go camp at the Sun Dance, but they would always take time out to come and get me."*

It is noteworthy that even now in the 1990's these ceremonies,
customs and social rules are still being practiced by some of our
people, especially in homes where tribal Medicine Bundles are
kept. This helps us to remain constantly aware of our ancient
faith and of our sacred duties in life. Other families in the tribe
no longer find the time or desire for such inherited devotions.
The majority of tribe members have respect for our tribal ways
even if they don't practice them in daily life.

When I was a child in my mother's house, the influences of
past people like her grandmother First-to-Kill were still very ap-
parent, though I didn't spend any time really thinking about it.
In fact, often I just saw my mother's ways as being very strict
when I wished they were not so (though now I'm glad of it!). I
too was expected to behave while indoors and not to "fool
around" in the presence of older people, especially medicine
people involved with sacred things. Although we had such people within our family, most kids of my generation missed out on
learning much about their sacred ways, which now makes me val-
ue my mother's experiences all the more.

*"Those old people that I grew up around used to talk a
lot about their bygone buffalo days. To them it was so
real, but not for me, so I didn't pay much attention. It
concerned a time and place that I never saw or experienced, so it just didn't mean much. Now that I am old
myself I think a lot more about those stories of the past -
I've come to long for something in them. That's why I
like to attend our Medicine Bundle ceremonies and tipi
camps whenever I can. I like to see people dress up for a
while in the way that my grandparents dressed most of
the time.*

*"I like to recall how my grandmother used to work stead-
ily to tan cow hides just as though they were buffalo from
back in the hunting days. She would make the same
kinds of things out of them - moccasins, bags, parfleches
and robes. By that time most of our people wore shoes
and store-bought clothing; they slept with sheets on met-
al-framed beds. My grandma and grandpa always stood
out in my mind for the way they remained faithful to their
original native way of life."*

The opportunities to experience our traditional native culture
the way that my mom is describing was fading around the time I
grew up in the 1950's. Here and there on the reservation lived the
last few old-timers who still wore long hair and moccasins.
Grandpa Heavy Head was about the last one who kept to his
breechcloth, though he pulled on trousers when strangers came
around or if he went somewhere else. Since then, those of us
committed to maintaining our tribal faith have had to base our
ways on more modern lifestyle experiences.

*"There's another unique thing about my grandmother
First-to-Kill that I like to remember, although I never
knew about this until I was older and going to school.
Even though she was a full blooded Indian woman of the
buffalo times, she spent about ten years of her life as a
young woman married to a German pioneer named Jo-*

*seph Trollinger, who came west and operated a hotel
and restaurant along the old Whoop-Up Trail, where it
crossed Mosquito Creek south of Calgary. During that
time she got baptized, legally married and answered to
the name of Lucy Trollinger, though she never really
learned to speak either German or English. An early
bishop travelling through the area was so impressed by
her cooking that he made note of it in his journal, which
was later published.*

*"It amazes me to think how this buffalo grandmother of
mine learned to cook and handle the work of such an es-
tablishment well enough to draw praise from a bishop.
The way I saw her years later as the wife of the medicine
man Heavy Head, it would be hard to picture her in the
other role. But she had proof in the five half-breed children that came from that union, including my mother,
Anadaki, or Pretty Woman.*

*"Actually, the way I found out about my German ancest-
ry was not very pleasant. It happened during one of my
first years at boarding school and it sure hurt my feelings. It's an example of how mean some people can be to
each other for no particular reason.*

*"The grandmother of one of my friends came to visit her
at school, where I spent most of each year after I turned
eight. Being curious like most kids, I went over to hear
what that old lady was saying to my friend. We were always eager to hear any news from our own people on the
"outside," since such topics weren't discussed otherwise
at the school, even though it was located right in the
midst of our reserve. This woman was another of the old-
time full-bloods like my grandmother, though she was
not so pleasant. She must not have liked me at all, for
she pointed at me in kind of a mean way and said to her
granddaughter, "Ones like her and her parents will be
the first ones to get kicked off this reserve when the half-
breeds lose their Indian rights."*

"She said all this in Blackfoot, but I understood her very

*well. The only part I couldn't figure out was why she meant **me** - I never thought of myself as a half-breed, my grandmother never told me about it. Sometime later when I was home I asked my mother, who then explained about the old lady having been for a while Mrs. Trollinger. She said when they finally split up, my grandmother came back to the reserve with her kids and got married to Heavy Head, who was unable to have children. He accepted these half-German kids as his own, and to me he was always my grandpa, even if we were not really of the same blood.*

"My grandfather Heavy Head was one of the gentlest men I've ever known. He really followed his traditions, partly for the fact that he went through the piercing ritual at the Sun Dance. He treated all people like his children when he was old. I never heard him raise his voice in anger.

"When my grandparents would be getting ready for a trip to town he would say to me, "What shall I bring back for you?' I would ask for candy, but he would say, 'Maybe you better pick something else, because we are not used to that kind of food and I don't want you to get sick from it!' We usually got apples and oranges for a treat instead."

The log house of my mother's parents, Joe and Hilda Beebe, looks small next to the two story home of her grandparents, Heavy Head and First-to-Kill, who lived right next door.
Collection of Good Medicine Foundation

My mother's comments on the animosity between full-bloods and mixed bloods points out one of the major challenges our people have had in trying to maintain a tribal identity while also learning non-tribal ways. Back in my parents' younger times our tribe's population had reached an all-time low, with less than two thousand members. The majority of these were full blooded, so that those with mixed ancestry really stood out. Favoring your own kind and being suspicious of "others" is a human trait as typical in native communities as anywhere else. Furthermore, mixed bloods generally had more school education and learned to understand white ways better, thus they managed to obtain positions of power, making the full-bloods feel left out. Thus there were periodic attempts to purge the tribe rolls of all but full bloods, though none of the efforts ever went very far. Nowadays the members of our tribe have intermarried with people from all races and nationalities. My father is among the few true full-bloods left, so this is no longer an important issue. I've met some of my own distant white relatives, who look about the same as some of my lightest cousins living on the reserve.

Still, the degree of "Indian-ness" among different families was a noticeable factor in social relationships between the kids of my generation when we went to school. Those who came from traditional families usually had a much harder time trying to catch onto the school's "white ways" than those of us who were raised in more mixed households. For instance, my mom's mother Anadaki, who was also called Hilda Strangling Wolf, was a major figure in my childhood, noted as a progressive woman in our tribe. Her first husband, Joe Beebe - my mom's dad - died when I was small.

> *"I was very close to my father Joe Beebe; I loved him very much. Because my parents lived next door to my grandparents, we all spent a lot of time together. Even now, from the windows of my own house I can see those places on the nearby prairie. Since then, I've raised my kids here too.*
>
> *"My father knew what it was like to live as an Indian - I*

*even have a picture of him wearing braids and mocca-
sins - but being a half breed he also knew how to get
around in the white world. He was a good farmer and
rancher, a good provider for his family. His father was a
Mormon named Joseph Beebe, whose father William Albert Beebe came to the U.S. from Scotland with the first
group of Mormons, the disciples of Brigham Young. I
never met this grandfather Beebe, but he was still a boy
when Brigham Young led the group to Utah. From there
Joseph Beebe eventually ran away, gave up his dad's
Mormon religion, then ended up among the Blood Indians in Canada. He worked in our country for many years
as a wagon driver, using oxen, mules and finally horses,
travelling mostly between Montana and Alberta. It so
happens that he often used the same road along which
my grandmother First-to-Kill and her white husband had
their stopping-over place. Eating one of her meals, he
had no idea that someday a son of his would marry a
daughter of theirs, and those are the ones who became
my parents.*

*"Joseph Beebe took Mountain Lion Woman for a wife,
and she became the mother of my father. Like my other
grandmother, she also grew up in a tipi during the buffalo days. In fact, she was still living in a tipi when they
met, although some of our people were beginning to try
log cabin life. The custom then was to give horses to the
parents when asking for their daughter, but since he
didn't have any horses he gave them money instead. This
was in the way of a very useful gift, though white people
sometimes misunderstood and thought the Indians were
"selling" their daughters.*

*"My father was born in a tipi that his parents shared, but
his mother died six days afterwards because she couldn't
discharge the afterbirth. Joseph Beebe wanted to bring a
white doctor from town, but the old midwives who were
attending her wouldn't allow it. In our customs, men
have no business around childbirths. As a result, the*

baby became sort of an orphan, living on an Indian re-
serve with a white wagoneer as widowed father. My dad's
Indian grandmother then took over and started to raise
him, bringing him from one mother to another to be
nursed. A strange thing about this was that she let him
nurse on her own breasts in between, until finally they
started giving a bit of milk themselves again, though at
her old age it probably wasn't much. Still, she was pretty
proud of this and let everyone know about it.

My mom's brother Howard Beebe (also known by his grand-
uncle's name, Bird Rattler), standing by his dad Joe (Red Tail-
feathers) and his mom Hilda (Pretty Woman).
Collection of Good Medicine Foundation

"Those were tough times for the Indians, soon after the
buffalo were gone, and there weren't a lot of choices for
food. Other babies were fed regularly from their mother's
breasts, but my dad had become quite undernourished.
Finally the old lady started spoon feeding him with
broths and he grew stronger. At seven his tipi life came to
an abrupt end when the old lady let him be taken away

to boarding school, where he stayed until graduating at
age eighteen. After that he became a scout and interpret-
er for the RCMP, until finally he settled down with my
mother and together they operated our ranch, here on
the Blood Indian Reserve in Southern Alberta.

The women who nursed my orphaned grandfather thought of
him from then on as a child of their own. One time, when I was a
young girl, an old man with braids asked me to interpret for him
to a storekeeper in town, so he could buy a few groceries. He
spoke only our Blackfoot language. When his buying was finished he asked me who I was, so I told him the names of my
grandparents. At that he smiled and said, "Oh, so you are my
granddaughter - I nursed from my mother along with your
grandfather Joe Beebe." Comments like that made a deep im-
pact on my sense of tribal identity and encouraged me to respect
other people even if they appear to be strangers.

> *"In my childhood I was surrounded by a lot of love from*
> *my parents and various grandparents. First-to-Kill and*
> *her husband Heavy Head lived right next door to us so I*
> *spent the most time with them, even though I've already*
> *said he wasn't my real grandfather. The way he treated*
> *me, it was just the same. Nearby lived another old couple*
> *whom I called grandma and grandpa, though the lady*
> *was actually my great-aunt and they had no children of*
> *their own. He would come down in his wagon to pick me*
> *up, saying, 'Your grandma has baked a pie for you,' so*
> *I'd get my belongings and go up to spend the night with*
> *them. He really loved children and always welcomed*
> *them at his home. The 'pie' usually turned out to be pan-*
> *fried bannock bread with currants or raisins in it.*
> *"This grandpa was named Red Leggings, and he was*
> *really protective of me. One time we were going on an*
> *overnight trip to Fort Macleod in their wagon. We*
> *camped along the way. I was dressed for town in the style*
> *of those days, including a good pair of long stockings.*

*But these got torn when I climbed down from the wagon
at this camp. Red Leggings scolded my grandma Coyote
Woman and told her she should have helped me, then he
climbed on a horse and rode the last few miles into town.
By that time the stores must have been closed, and Red
Leggings couldn't speak English to go shopping any-
way, but he wasn't going to have his granddaughter embarrassed the next day by going around with torn stockings, so he managed to get me a new pair somehow. He
gave them to me the next morning, and I recall that being a pretty impressive thing to my young mind.*

"My grandparents doctored me with their Indian medi-
cines whenever I got sick and there was no white doctor
nearby. They also showed me their faith in other old customs, for example their cure for nightmares. I learned
this on another trip to Fort Macleod that I made with
them, in two wagons - Heavy Head and First-to-Kill in
one, with Red Leggings and Coyote Woman in the other.
We went to get fresh cow intestines from the slaughter-
house - for the old folks this was a delicacy left over from
buffalo days. They had different ways of stuffing and
cooking them, and gladly made this long trip just to sat-
isfy their tastes.

"We were camped along the river bottom at Fort Macleod, where my grandparents washed and prepared their
old-time food while I ran around and played. I suddenly
came upon a big snake that was black and red and
scared me quite a lot. It seemed to attack me, then it went
off into the water, while I screamed and ran back to my
grandparents. That night I kept having nightmares about
it, so finally old Red Leggings got up, took a coal from
the stove as if making incense, then he took some of the
fur from an old buffalo hide that we travelled with and
he place this on top of that coal. The smoke took away
my bad dreams and I slept good after that. These are
things I still remember from those old-time people more
than seventy years afterwards."

Imagine the great change for my mother, moving from her simple life with old time Indians to a strict Catholic institution run by white men and women who never had children of their own. Her grandparents made sure she enjoyed her childhood, so they didn't burden her with chores. Our native customs allow a child to learn by watching, going at his or her own pace, eventually showing what's been learned by example. From such an environment my mom moved one day to school where the learning was strict, hard, and enforced with deadlines and tests that took no account of a child's natural development. For some, the conflicting pressures led to problems in adult life that include alcohol and family violence, though most of my mother's generation learned eventually to combine the two different ways into practical philosophies and customs that are still working and evolving today.

Red Leggings and Coyote Woman, a couple who treated my mom like a real granddaughter, though this lady was actually her great-aunt. The picture was taken in 1913, just a few years before my mom started visiting in their household.
Collection of Good Medicine Foundation

A mother and daughter, dressed up for a special occasion. This woman was the wife of Sweetgrass, brother of my mom's grand-ma First-to-Kill. Women of the Blackfoot Confederacy can go through a special ceremony in which they are given the right to wear an eagle feather headdress, generally worn only by chiefs and warriors. Her daughter not only wears a fine buck-skin dress, an elaborate bead breastplate, and fully beaded leg-gings, but she also has on a horned weasel headdress. It was probably transferred to her by some old warrior as a symbol of good luck, and evidence that she was a traditionally "favoured child." Behind them stands the 'Big Stripe' tipi, one of numer-ous painted lodges that used to identify Blackfoot tipi camps. Collection of Glenbow Archives

2.

"Going to Sit"
A Native View of Schooling

Attending to boarding school was sort of a love-hate experi-ence for many generations of Indian children, including my mom and later myself. Actually, my grandmother Anadaki was the first in our family line to be sent to such a school, but the system in the 1890's was then just being set up so it operated on more or less of a voluntary basis. By my mom's time in the 1920's things had become so strict that every child was required to leave home and board at school, with priests and government authorities going around the reserve to find those who didn't show up on their own. Our tribe was host to two religious de-nominations - the Roman Catholics and the Anglicans - who ac-tually vied with each other for the young of our tribe, whom they considered morally doomed unless they were given the severe in-doctrination that was expected to turn them from ordinary Indi-ans into "civilized" and God-fearing wards of the government.

> *"Education for us Indian children in those days meant staying in school day and night for many years. Actually, the reserve schools only took us to grade eight, and only some of us got that far. But we had to stay until we were 16, since there were many other things for us to learn in boarding school besides the lessons in classrooms. They attempted to teach us a complete way of making a living.*
> *"A child had to be seven before starting school, al-though some were quite a bit older before they got around to the first grade. Then at sixteen they had to leave school, no matter how smart they were or how well they were doing, though during my time they raised that age to eighteen. Whether we learned very much or not depended a great deal on the nature of our teacher. If*

we were fortunate to get a good-hearted person, he or
she would try very hard to have us understand. It took
*the character of a **real person** to put in all their willpow-*
er, to honestly try helping these Indian children get
somewhere further with their education.

When my mother speaks of someone as a "real person," that is
a strong statement, since in our Blackfoot language natives are
called Nitsitapi, or Real People. It has been one of the unfortu-
nate drawbacks to life on Indian reservations that we have often
gotten those kinds of teachers, doctors, nuns and others who were
possibly not quite good enough to work somewhere more important than among an impoverished tribe like ours. Such people
often showed us their frustrations, or even blamed us for their
own shortcomings. In turn, the Indian people have generally rec-
ognized these individuals for what they were, but did their best to
accommodate them. However, they were not the ones considered
worthy of being called "real persons."

It is only fair to say at this time that there were many others
who came gladly to work with Indian people, more so in the recent "era of enlightenment," starting in the 1960's. I should also
mention that nowadays we have many members within our tribes
qualified as teachers, nurses, even professors, so we are able to
teach ourselves in addition to whatever we learn from others.

"When a child was sent off to school we referred to it in
our Blackfoot language as "going to sit." When the old-
time people visited with each other they would say, 'He
has gone to make his children sit,' meaning some father
went and enrolled his kids at the boarding school.
"At first they were still given the privilege of speaking
Blackfoot, to make the break from their families easier,
since most usually spoke no other language. They were
given a period of time - say about a month - to learn
some English words. Of course, the teacher would talk to
them in English right off, since he or she wouldn't know
any Blackfoot. By the second month in school the child

> *was compelled to speak nothing but English; after that*
> *any use of the Indian language was strictly forbidden.*
> *This was very hard for us children; any chance we had*
> *by ourselves - even if the teacher just stepped briefly out*
> *of the room - we'd all talk to each other in Blackfoot.*
> *But then there would be stool pigeons amongst us and*
> *they would tell, saying 'so and so was talking in Black-*
> *foot,' and we'd get punished for it. That's how it was for*
> *the whole nine years that I remained in school. But now-*
> *adays life has come so far that things are turned right*
> *around, with most of our Indian children knowing noth-*
> *ing but English and the teachers at school wanting them*
> *to learn Blackfoot."*

Learning to live with a new language was a major challenge
for kids in our tribe going to school right up to my own time
during the late 1950's. I had learned English around my family
by then, although Blackfoot was our main tongue, but I sure felt
sorry for those kids among us who were unable to speak English
at all. They had a much harder time adjusting to our new system.
I clearly recall a drawing on our first classroom wall that showed
a white child yelling into a megaphone: "If you *must* speak
Blackfoot, whisper." It was no longer totally forbidden, as in my
mom's time, but the nuns made sure we felt badly about it. They
would have abhorred the idea that someday students in those
same classrooms would receive credit for relearning their own
tongue.

> *"Right the next day after I arrived at boarding school I*
> *was made to go work in the kitchen. They showed me a*
> *small area to wash and keep clean behind the cookstove.*
> *I also had to go get kindling wood and put it in a certain*
> *place where it would be ready for the man who worked in*
> *the boiler room; he also made fire in the big cookstove in*
> *the kitchen. He started the fire with that kindling and*
> *then he put in coal, which was our main fuel. Every*
> *morning I did the same thing, bringing that kindling*

*wood and then washing real good behind the stove. I
don't know how big that stove was, but it sure seemed
long and huge to me. It had two main sections - one for
the regular cooking and another one for making cakes.
That was my work for the first whole month in school; it
was my first real taste of the white man's world, and I
have not forgotten it since.*

**What a contrast for a girl born to family life in log cabins, ti-
pis, and the outdoors. What turmoil was in the mind of this
young student peeling potatoes, and what righteous thoughts
accompanied the child-less nun at the stove, who saw native
ways only in negative terms, with no first-hand experience or
understanding.**
Provincial Archives of Alberta Photograph Collection

Although the Blood tribe has the largest reservation in Canada,
its location in southwestern Alberta is away from the mainstream
of North American society, so that in my mother's time it was
still common for kids to grow up with little outside influence.
Into the 1930's and 40's there were numbers of pre-school
Blackfoot kids who considered it normal to wear braids and
moccasins all the time. But this was over by my time in the 50's,

so our arrival at boarding school was not so traumatic. We'd had a fair bit of contact with the white world already - going to town with our parents, even travelling to other tribes and places. Unfortunately, these journeys often included racially-motivated experiences, so that I entered school basically scared of "white men," and also of their "white ladies."

The strict boarding school era was slowly coming to a close when my turn came to enter it, but there are strong impressions left on my mind from those days of being "institutionalized." For instance, from the start we had to make our beds properly, in military style. I think because of this I now sometimes leave my bed unmade, as a symbol that I'm free.

Another memory of my first days at boarding school makes me chuckle whenever I think about it. When we arrived, all our personal clothing from home was collected, each sewn into brown paper bags with our names attached. At the end of the school year we received our clothing back. This one year somebody played a little trick and switched the names on two of the bags, so that a girl in my class found a pair of long combination underwear while one of the boys down the hall pulled out some panties and a slip. It was a good year-end story for the whole school, and it was told all over the reservation, besides.

> *"Let me recall a typical day for us at boarding school in the 1920's . Early in the morning we were awakened by the supervising nun, who came into the dormitory and rang a bell that was kept at one end of the wash stand. When we heard that bell we sat right up in bed, and then the nun would lead us in prayer.*
> *"Only after we said this prayer did we dare touch our feet to the floor, and then we went right to our place at the long wash stand, got out our basins and filled them with a bit of hot water, then we washed up. Two girls shared a dish of soap, and with this soap we washed our faces and our teeth. Like all our other things, this soap had our identification numbers on it.*
> *"After we finished at the sink we went to make our beds*

*and get dressed. If the bed was just a tiny bit messy the
nun would make us do it over again. We had to fold and
tuck the sheets and spreads in a certain way, and also to
fold our clothes neatly on the chair next to us. When we
were finished and dressed we sat down on our chairs and
waited for the rest to get done. Then we were called over
to the wash stand, this time to kneel down and again
pray together. We'd say the Our Father, a Hail Mary, the
Apostle's Creed, the four acts of Faith, Hope and Chari-
ty, plus an act of contrition. At this time we always
prayed for our parents, too. Then we went down two by
two and entered the chapel, where we prayed some more.
This time we were together with the whole school - the
boys on the right side and the girls on the left; the older
ones sat in front and the smaller ones further back. When
we took our places the priest came in and said mass. We
could go to communion also if we wanted, but this part
was left to our choice, except on certain days when we all
went.*

*"After mass was finished we went downstairs to the play-
room. There we found our coverall aprons, which were
hung up in a row with our numbers on them. We put
these on, then those of us assigned to help in the dining
room went down to get the tables ready, after which the
rest came down for breakfast, again at the ringing of a
bell. The boys had a separate dining room from the girls.
As soon as we finished our meals we were sent to our assigned jobs, whether it was in the kitchen, dining room,
or laundry. When that work was finished we had to show
it to the nun in charge, and if she was satisfied then we
could go back down to the playroom, until it was time for
classes to start at nine.*

Like a military troop, three nuns have lined up their Blood Indian girl students out in front of St. Mary's Catholic Residential School, where many members of my family have attended. My mother, who was then about 12 years old, is standing almost directly above the center nun.
Collection of Good Medicine Foundation

"The boys had a classroom and we girls had our own. For the next three hours we had the typical three R kind of schooling, then at noon we went back to the dining room for lunch. After eating, the nun would check our dresses to see if our stockings and garters were in place and without holes. We also had to show that we hadn't lost our handkerchiefs, which were kept in pockets that they sewed near the hems of our petticoats.

"In the afternoons we continued with our classroom studies until four, then we were sent to work to different parts of the school, such as the kitchen, until 5:30. Those assigned to the dining room would then go and get the tables ready, while the rest of us waited in the playroom for the bell to ring, at which time we went for supper. After that we all went to the chapel, even the school staff,

where we said the rosary together. Then we had some
time to play - outside if it was good weather - except that
those with dining room assignments had to go back and
clean up. At 8:00 each evening the supervising nun rang
the bell and we had to go in and get ready for bed.
"As you can see, we were totally dependant on these
nuns and school people from morning till night, which is
why I get very disturbed these days when I hear in the
news about so many of them having supposedly abused
children. We all assumed that they were practicing what
they had preached, and it is quite a shock now to learn
that some were doing otherwise.
"In fact, one of my earliest conflicts with life was the re-
sult of these school people acting so superior to us. They
taught us that our native ways were evil and this upset
me very much. I dearly loved my grandparents, but at
school we were told that the traditional ways they were
following would cause them to burn in the everlasting
fires of hell. I didn't want this to happen to them - they
were so gentle and kind. My grandpa never even raised
his voice and he was like this to all people. Yet from what
they were saying in school he was really evil and bad.
For a long time I couldn't make sense out of these con-
tradictions."

Further to my mother's words, I would say in hindsight that
the churches were very helpful to the *physical* needs of us Indian
children when they brought us to their schools - whether in my
mom's time or my own - providing us with safe roofs, healthy
foods and warm clothing, back in a time when Indian families
were generally poor and often found it hard to provide these
things. But on the *spiritual* and *emotional* level I'd say they
nearly destroyed us. We lived constantly in fear of this new god
of theirs, who would send people to hell at the drop of a hat. The
way this was told to us - using our tribal ways and old people as
supposedly evil examples - made us feel pretty bad about ourselves. I can't help wondering how good things might have

turned out if only these people had treated us with more open-hearted understanding.

Misunderstandings affected our whole culture, not just our religious ways. For instance, we consider it unwise to scare little children, and when they are scared we try to comfort them. During one of my first years at boarding school we were shown a feature movie that had scary parts - rented films had by that time become part of our isolated school's regular entertainment. Afterwards we had a hard time to sleep in our big dark room, so the girl in the bunk below me decided we'd sleep together and comfort our fright. Next morning I awoke to a slap in the face from a nun, after which I was pulled from the bed by my hair, the insinuation being that we did something immoral.

Another time they tried to scare us at school but I was much older and found it very funny. The feature film they had rented for us was "Dracula," and the first time he appeared on the screen someone jumped out on the stage and into the crowd wearing a mask and cape, at which point pandemonium broke out among the little kids, who were screaming and falling over their chairs trying to head for the back door. Just about every time the vampire appeared in the film this caped character would come out and everyone would scramble, then they'd have to stop the film and turn the lights on till everyone had their nerves back and their chairs up. As I've said already, by my time the strictness of early boarding school days was coming to an end.

"Those nuns and priests practically replaced our parents once we got into school, and this was even more so after we girls turned fourteen. They didn't want us to get involved with boys, so at that age they no longer allowed us to leave school even in the summertime, until we were ready to get married. Everything we learned about living came from school, whether it was discipline and studies, or making such things as soups and fruitcakes, doing the sewing and laundry, even getting our own food from the school's garden and farm animals. You name it and we probably learned it there.

*"This was the loneliest time of my life, during those sum-
mers when almost everyone else got to go home. There
were only about twenty of us girls who were kept back.
But they made sure we stayed busy, doing chores around
the school and farm such as milking the cows, churning
the butter, tending the gardens and so forth. One special
treat was that the nuns often made themselves extra
breakfast so we could have the leftovers, including such
things as ham and eggs which we never got during the
rest of the year. Also, once a week or so we were taken to
the river for swimming or to pick wild berries.*

*"One interesting result of my being separated for so long
from my mother was that I lost the ability to call her 'Na-
ah,' which is our Blackfoot term of endearment between
child and mother. I guess I became embarrassed of that
word, so for most of my life I called her Anadaki, Pretty
Crow Woman, which was her Indian name. Not until my
old age, during my mother's final years, did I feel comfortable calling her as I did in my childhood, 'Na-ah.'"*

The boarding school era in Indian history has received a lot of
justified criticism, especially in recent times by younger people
looking back. Yet surprisingly neither my mother nor many others of her generation carry bitter thoughts or feelings about their
school years nor about those who were in charge of them. She
has often said that the strictness helped her learn skills and values
that she used in raising her own family. The only thing she does
still resent is the attitudes shown not only by the school people,
but also by society at large towards us native Indians, as though
we were rather ignorant, like wild animals that had to be tamed,
our spirits completely broken so we'd be easier to lead around.
In more recent years she has been pleasantly surprised by the
growing interest and respect that mainstream society is showing
for traditional Indian ways. Her enthusiasm for this process is
one reason she has urged me to compile this book.

*My mom and dad were in this crowd that posed for the official
grand opening of the St. Mary's Catholic Residential School
in 1927, but they didn't really know each other and had no idea
yet that they'd get married and spend over 60 years of their
lives together. My father, Ed Little Bear, is kneeling in front,
second from right. My mom is way up on the balcony, second
row behind the Union Jack flag, second right from the middle
white post. Among the foreground dignitaries are the Catholic
bishop and our long-time head chief Shot-on-Both-Sides, the
only two men sitting down.*
Atterton Photo. Collection of Glenbow Archives

3.

Seeing Boarding School from the Other Side

It was like looking at someone else's diaries, somebody you knew pretty intimately, writing about things that concerned you. That's how I felt a few times in recent years when I've gone to some library or archives and read through the papers of government agents, priests, nuns and inspectors who were seeing our people and tribal ways through their own eyes. I even knew some of these people, but was too young to understand their actual work and purpose. Reading them now gives me a whole new perspective on past events not only in my life but also that of my parents.

Growing up in a conservative tribe whose members were still quite suspicious of outsiders, I heard many rumors and stories concerning the various church and government people with whom we had our daily dealings. Just as they no doubt spoke harshly about us at times when we weren't listening, so our people did about them, usually in Blackfoot and generally quite freely.

Unfortunately our people had no access to church and government records to dispel the many rumors that have proven to be false. Also, those who were in charge of our affairs often assumed natives were ignorant and not worth the effort needed to explain to them their own affairs. This I've found to be especially true while reading papers from back in the earlier reservation years, say around 1900, when none of our chiefs and leaders could speak English, thus were unable to demonstrate to these outsiders their deep thinking ways and fine oratorical abilities. By the time mixed blood translators worked over their speeches the interpretations often sounded crude and awkward, with the real messages lost.

Of course, it is true that our traditional tribal philosophy was much different from the kinds of thoughts the outsiders wanted us to have, or adopt. Even if the outsiders had understood Blackfoot they would have been baffled by some of what those old chiefs said. But time has shown the values of our natural wisdom - on hindsight it would have been better if church and government people had given up most of *their* ways and learned to follow ours. If you understand how well our old ways functioned in harmony with nature, then you can appreciate why our chiefs and people were so unwilling to accept the imposed changes.

To give you a better idea of how the church and government people of past years talked about their "Indian wards," here are some excerpts from Inspector's Reports which were sent to their head office from the Blood Reserve. You can follow the slow pace of acceptance by our people as the years go along. These papers are now at the National Archives in Ottawa:

> 1898   *"Students cannot be had in any numbers....The parents do not like the idea of pupils being held till 18 years of age....It seems a pity that a school costing over $3,000 should be built and allowed to stand empty.....*
>
> 1899   *"Eight pupils are now attending.....Sister St. Germain is in charge.*
>
> 1900   *"Fourteen boys and five girls enrolled... Two classes: Book and Second Book. Some students speak English with a French accent due to French teachers, although instruction is in English.*
>
> *"One boy sick with open sores; recommend sending him to Calgary for treatment as none is available on Blood Reserve.*
>
> *"Without treatment, government will be wasting money to educate one who in a few years will be dead, or a useless burden to himself and those connected with him."*
>
> *Indian Affairs in Ottawa responds to the above:*
> *"If Department's instructions were properly fol-*

lowed, no scrofulous pupils would be admitted to such schools, as they are a menace to other students as well as a bill of expense to the Department."

1901   *"It seems a pity more children cannot be gotten to fill up vacant rooms. There are lots on the Reserve but they are hard to get."*

1903   *"Iron beds are used at the Catholic Boarding School on Blood Agency. Each bed has mattress, sheets, blankets, quilt and pillow and more blankets in winter when required. There is a good sized kitchen and excellent range. Dining room has three large tables and one small one. There is a neat little chapel on the second floor.*
Work in the class is fairly satisfactory. Pupils read very well and were fair at arithmetic. Neatly dressed...."

1905   *21 boys and 17 girls. Father LaVerne, OMI, was principal.*

1906   *Staff salaries at Mission school, per annum:*
Fr. Salaun (principal) - $400
Sister Marjorie (matron) - $300
Sr. Patrick (senior teacher) - $250
Cook, seamstress, attendants, etc. - $200.
20 boys and 26 girls; Grades I - IV
"I put an item of $100 for fire escapes and another $100 for painting in the current year's estimates for this school, but they were struck out at Ottawa."

1910   *Buildings flooded to ground floor in 1908. 20 girls and 19 boys. $29 received in prizes by children at Macleod Exhibition, including $5 by one boy for a watercolor.*

1911   *45 children; 23 boys from 6-16; 22 girls from 7-15.*

1912   *Two new pupils admitted; three transferred to Dunbow Industrial School.*

"The school gave the usual Indian Christmas feast at which about 300 Indians were present on Dec. 24, 1912."

"This school has the champion hockey team of this country, having beaten all comers."

1913   *"Peter Black Rabbit, Joe Crazy Crow, Peter Short Man and Hairy Bull all transferred to Dunbow. Jim Many Feathers, Black Eagle, Paula Riding in the Door and Louisa Plaited Hair absent all month."*

1913   *"The boys from this school have gone to their respective homes for their summer holidays." (August)*

"Pupils won $38.50 at Macleod Fair. Mary White Calf discharged after marriage to Henry Big Throat. Holidays ended on 14th, but by Sept. 3rd not returned were: Long-Time Squirrel, Paul Melting Tallow, Jas. Takes Gun Strong, Francis Black Eagle and the two Snake Eater boys."

1917   35 boys and 27 girls.

"The children of the Blood Indians have not of late years impressed me as being very bright or quick to take up their studies. The teachers seem to be interested in their work and are doubtless doing their best.....

"I have thought the minds of the children were too much engrossed in the society doings on the reserve to give the attention to their studies that is necessary to make rapid advancement. The pupils at both of the schools here are in too close touch with reserve events, I think."

Two horses and three cows are kept for the school. About 4 acres cultivated; 400 bushels of potatoes and 100 bushels of turnips were harvested.

1922   60 pupils

"Sister Gertrude succeeds in getting her class

*through the reading lesson by half pronouncing
the word, the pupil following up and appending
the tails. In this manner each pupil reads once
and then the class is dismissed. Spelling is taken
orally, each pupil getting one word to spell. In
arithmetic in Grade III the method is to call the
class. All face the front of the room, then the
teacher goes to a side board and sets down this
question:*

$$96573 \\ \underline{\quad x\,4}$$

*One pupil is sent to the board to work the prob-
lem. He multiplies aloud, setting down the figures
as he does so. His position is such that the rest of
the class cannot observe what he is doing without
turning around. And this they do not do, hence
taking no more part in the recitations than do the
inhabitants of Mars.*

*"Sister Mary's instruction is defective in every re-
spect. Class management, supervision, assignments and methods of presenting the work are la-
mentably poor. In art and needlework the
children are good."*

1922   *"These Indian schools are the biggest farce to be
called schools I have ever seen. They appear to
be all pretty much the same. Teachers who are
about the poorest of their class are in charge,
and the waste of time is painful to witness. What
crime have these children committed that they
should be imprisoned from nine o'clock until
four with little else to do than suck their thumbs a
major portion of the time. Any good teacher
should teach these pupils as much in half an
hour as under the present conditions they are
taught all day....   I have seen some very crude
teaching, but I think I can safely say that I have
never before seen .... anything put forward as*

> *teaching that touched quite such a low level as*
> *that which is to be seen in these Indian schools.*"

Apparently the man who made these strong statements was normally the Inspector of Public Schools in Alberta, a provincial official with an unfriendly outlook on schools paid for by the federal government, and for the use of only specific groups of people. The following reply was sent to the Deputy Superintendent General of Indian Affairs in Ottawa by Father Joseph Guy, O.M.I., an important Catholic official at the University of Ottawa. These are some extracts from his lengthy defense.

> "*Rev. Fr. E. Ruaux O.M.I., Principal of Blood R.C. Indi-*
> *an Boarding School, has received from the Department*
> *the order to effect complete change in the teaching staff*
> *of the institution. The reasons brought forward state that*
> *the teachers do not possess sufficient instruction nor the*
> *necessary pedagogical qualities. The Rev. Principal has*
> *simply been startled by the departmental communication*
> *and has requested me to protest in his name against what*
> *he calls unfair treatment.*
> "*Rev. Fr. Ruaux is more than surprised at the hastiness*
> *of the Department in taking action after only one inspec-*
> *tion and only one report from an inspector who showed*
> *not even the slightest knowledge of Indian children nor*
> *seemed to possess the least idea of the difficulties met*
> *with in the education of young Indians.*
> "*Regarding the allegation that the teachers do not pos-*
> *sess the required degree of instruction, Rev Fr. Ruaux*
> *denies it most emphatically stating:*
> *1.   that Sr. Ste Gertrude has received the Model Cer-*
> *   tificate of Quebec Normal School in English and*
> *   French, together with two other certificates from*
> *   United States schools.*
> *2.   that Sr. Ste Marie though not in possession of*
> *   any Normal School certificate has received a very*
> *   good English training in U. S. schools and en-*

3.

*joys a rather valuable experience as a teacher;
....(the Inspector) had the ingenuity to admit to
Rev. Fr. Ruaux that he entertained great doubts
of his success with the Indian children, whose
whole appearance, by the way, he found stupid
rather than intelligent (as he now says). He probably did not realize that his abundance of words
was practically unintelligible to the children,
many of whom not being sufficiently familiarized
with the English language.... The Rev. Principal
ends by stating that he does not intend to change
the teaching staff....."*

This exchange is a good example of how our people were regularly used as pawns by various groups and individuals who had
something to gain from their control over us. In this case, the
priest and nuns mentioned were from the schooling days of my
parents, who have nothing but good to say about them, recalling
them as "real people" who tried their best to understand us and
help us out.

It is true that nuns sent to the Bloods and other Blackfeet were
often French-speaking, so the English they taught us was sometimes rough. To this day you can identify former students of the
various schools among us by the way they talk English; more
than a few have strong hints of French mixed in. But my dad
knew this Sister St. Gertrude - he says in Blackfoot she was called
Heavy Nose Sister - and he thinks she spoke English quite well.
The mention of Father Ruaux made my parents recall the following incident, which gives some idea of how they thought of him.

*"There were two boys in our school, one named Albert
and the other Eugene, who were known for being naugh-
ty and getting in trouble. One time they got hold of some
of the sisters' habits and dressed themselves up as nuns.
They went outside to one end of the schoolyard and they
started walking back and forth, each with a prayer book
in his hand, acting like they were studying the bible.*

*They probably did this to be able to stay out of class.
Well, Father Ruaux noticed them and said something in
French, to which one of them answered, "Oui monsieur,"
but they kept walking. On their way back he said something in French to them again, but got the same answer,
"Oui, Monsieur." At this point the Father got suspicious
so he went over to take a closer look and here it was Albert and Eugene. Well those boys hiked up their skirts
and started to run, with Father Ruaux right behind trying to kick their rear ends. But the whole time he was
laughing so hard that he'd have to stop and take a
breather, then chase after them again. The whole school
got a lot of laughs out of it."*

**Students attending St. Mary's School during the time of my
parents dreaded this particular view, showing Father Ruaux at
his desk, because it usually meant they were in trouble and had
been sent to "the Principal's office." His calendar says Febru-
ary 1927, so both my parents were probably in nearby classrooms. Like all outsiders who stayed among our people for any
length of time, Father Ruaux was given an Indian name; thus,
in the Blackfoot language he was known as Eagle Horn.**
Collection of Good Medicine Foundation

4.

My Mother's Arranged Marriage

The desire to control our people reached one of its extremes during the era of my mom's schooling, when maturing girls were no longer allowed to leave school and go home at all until they were ready to marry an approved husband. The idea was apparently to put the most educated and ambitious boys and girls together so that they might succeed and set examples for other people, in itself perhaps a laudable goal, but again done without regard for our own traditions and culture.

The authorities probably didn't know that their strict demands on these young people were not actually that much different from the way marriages were arranged in our customs. From stories told by my grandmothers of the buffalo era, girls of marriageable age were strictly watched by their mothers and aunts. Blackfoot custom places great regard on the virtuousness of the tribe's girls, whose husbands were usually chosen by their parents and family - often with the goal of matching wise and ambitious young people. Within our tribal society that custom was still the norm in my mother's time, except that the priests then also demanded influence in the selection and insisted on giving final approval.

> *"Eventually the time came for me to leave school and get married. The 1920's were over and we were into the 'hungry thirties,' which were tough times for everybody - white and Indian. In those days our parents still chose our husbands, so my father was starting to look around at the eligible young men. But I told him that this was too embarrassing for me; I didn't think too highly of myself and so I was afraid that his request for someone to marry me would be turned down. I had made kind of a*

pledge to myself that I wasn't going to look around for a
husband nor let my parents look for me - I wanted to just
wait and see who would come and ask for my hand. Also,
I was afraid he might marry me into a rich family and I
considered myself too poor for that.

"Your dad's aunt came to me one day at the school and
said her nephew was in favour of marrying nobody else
except me. We were not friends of any kind - I knew him,
but we had nothing in common. Still, I was agreeable
and so were my parents, so we all talked to the priest and
he gave his approval. He could have turned us down;
when he's asked in these situations, he knows the boy
and girl, knows what they are like, so he decides from
that if they are suitable. Since your dad went to the same
school - just a little ahead of me - the priest was satisfied
and the arrangements were made.

"Your dad and I had two visits together before we got
married, that's all. The priest made arrangements for a
certain part of the dining area at the school, and that's
where we got to speak and visit, for an hour each time.
Other than that I had never spoken to your dad, just seen
him from the distance. In those days maybe one or two
girls out of a hundred was in love with the same man she
was going to marry.

"Six of us couples got married at the same time, on
Christmas Eve of 1934. Two had already been living together for a while in our native custom, but four of us
schoolgirls were finally leaving the boarding school. Be-
forehand, the priest gave us some instructions about life
and marriage; the nuns also helped us get ready. We
sewed quilts and clothes, even our own wedding dresses.
We used them both for graduation and for getting married."

In 1984 my parents celebrated their fiftieth wedding anniver-
sary at the same school and church where they got started, and
there was quite a large crowd on hand. Although they hardly

knew each other at first, they *did* fall in love with each other a long, long time ago. They were given more say about their proposed marriage than many couples of the buffalo days, yet they still basically followed an old native custom by getting married first, then working on their bonds of love.

Freedom at Last! Rolled papers signifying graduation from boarding school for my mom (on the left) and three friends, Eva (Vielle) Prairie Chicken, Jane (Russell) Davis, and Annie (Blood) Bare Shin Bone. Having made their own graduation dresses, they soon got further use from them when all four got married. From here they went back to reservation life, struggling to combine what they learned in school with our own tribal customs and beliefs.
Clarke Photo. Collection of Good Medicine Foundation

Thoughtful parents seeking a mate for their daughter or son usually checked first to see how that individual treated his or her parents, as an indication of their character and personality. Generosity was also a very important factor - a good son-in-law gave his wife's parents choice meat from his hunts and horses or other goods from his war raids. A good daughter-in-law cooked delicacies for her husband's parents and made things like moccasins, especially for his father. Still, if a daughter was strongly against her parents' choice for a mate, they generally gave up and sought for another one.

"Fortunately, I didn't lose my Indian ways during those years that I spent at school. It's strange, but you don't let go of them, inside. As soon as you get back out, when you meet with your grandparents that you've hardly seen in a long time, it all comes right back to you. They begin to tell you about the things you've missed out on, the camps and ceremonies and gatherings, then you quickly get back into it. That's the social life of our people.

"For instance, I quickly got back to making things like berry soup, dried meats, pemmican and other Indian foods. After marriage we first stayed with your father's family where the head of the household was old Eagle Plume and his two wives, who were every bit as traditional as my own grandparents and of an even older generation. I picked up a lot of things from them, traditional ways that I hadn't learned at all in school. For instance, when I cooked for them they would tell me the ways they wanted their food done, or they'd show me their old time methods, so I knew how to cook for people both in the old way and the new.

"Now take today, a young person usually learns things just from a book, or by watching instead of doing; this is the way they teach them, right through university. You choose an occupation of some kind and you study only that; it will be your life. But they will not teach you how to make your own living, how to feed yourself and so forth. If I meet with a person who has five years of university, they will talk very smart but they won't know how to do anything practical for themselves. I believe we learned way more from our simple elders than what they learn in all the years at their modern schools."

One conflict for my mother between old ways and new would probably have surprised the church people if they'd known. We Indians of today often blame churches and "the white man" for making us lose our culture, forbidding our religion and so forth. My mother's grandfather Heavy Head, the one she speaks of as being really kind and holy, often told her not to get involved in the ceremonial ways that he so fully believed in. Wise old ones like him saw that if their younger people kept on being so much different from white society, they'd have a hard time supporting their families and getting a fair deal. They often encourage white ways instead, figuring it was the only way their people would become equal, something that is slowly coming true in recent years. Another reason spiritual leaders like Heavy Head discouraged the young from getting too involved is that our Blackfoot ways are very complex, demanding, powerful, and easy to mishandle. Realizing the young understood little of the ancient life, they didn't want to witness a mishandling of the ceremonies that go with it. According to tribal teachings, such mishandling could have grave consequences.

In spite of these concerns there have always been enough people in each generation to pass on the core of our Blackfoot ways, right up to this time. It is ironic how church people and their preaching are often criticized today for being out of touch with society - as they used to say of us - while the native ways and beliefs such as Heavy Head practiced are now said by many to give hope for our future. On the Blood Reserve we are still basically Indians, whereas the missionaries and government agents have come and gone.

"When we moved in with your dad's family, his uncle gave him a wagon and a team of horses, with harness, and they gave me a very old fashioned type of sewing machine. This uncle, Willie Eagle Plume, had adopted your dad after your grandfather died. He also gave your dad the proceeds of ten acres of his land, in return for helping with the family farm work. This amounted to about $200, which was a lot of money at that time. With it he bought a saddle, a bed and some other things.

"So that was the start of our married life, living with old Eagle Plume's family and the Many Children clan, who were also called the Small Robes. The older women started teaching me the etiquette of married women accord-

ing to our own tribal customs, which I missed out on learning while I was at school. For instance, I was told never to interfere with men's talk. 'When men are talking business, just listen,' they told me, 'or better yet, go in the next room.' That was their way; I learned it especially from my new mother-in-law, your dad's uncle's wife. She had been previously married to a very strict man who taught her things the hard way.

"I was told never to sing along if the men were singing Indian songs; that was not considered proper for a woman. Today you hear a lot of Indian women singing along with the men - even beating on the drums - but that was not allowed in our old traditions. It was kind of hard for me, since back in school we had been fairly free to say whatever we wanted, or to sing. I eventually did join your dad with some of his Indian singing; he encouraged me to do it, though I never beat on the drum."

If this makes my mom sound like she just took orders while staying in the background, I should mention that she was too strong-willed for that. She accepted this role while staying with my dad's family, who were strict full-bloods known for being conservative. After my parents moved out on their own, she generally conducted all our family business such as shopping and banking, even buying cars, though she herself never drove anything other than wagons and buggies. When my dad worked for others, he just handed the money over to her; she always controlled the purse strings.

"At this time I had an old grandfather named Bird Rattler who was living down on the Blackfeet Reservation in Montana. He and his wife, Gets Water, lived alone with their little grandson James Boy, so we moved down there to help them out. We had very little of our own yet, so it was a good thing for us as well as for the old folks. Our first child William was just a baby, so three of us made the move down to the U.S.."

This grandfather of my mother's was almost a legendary person in our family, sort of a hero since the time I can first remember. He was one of the last great warriors among all the Blackfoot people, both in the U.S. and Canada, a man of special pride and honor. Actually, he was my mother's grand-uncle, the brother of her father's mother Mountain Lion Woman, though in Indian custom that makes him a grandfather. He was originally a Blood from Canada, like the rest of our family, but he got into trouble with the Mounted Police and that's how he ended up down in the States. He had been caught coming back from a horse raid after that was forbidden. It didn't keep him from being a very highly respected man in his old age, a tribal judge and a ceremonial leader. He was also fairly well off for an old-time Indian, so he took care of my parent's basic needs in return for the help and company they provided. They were following an old custom, whereby newlyweds live with older relatives until they have enough resources to set up their own household.

"Because your dad was Bird Rattler's son-in-law by our customs, we couldn't stay in the same house with them. There was still way too much respect for that. Instead, we lived in a little shed that sat next to the main house. It had a cookstove and a lot of cupboards; not ordinary cupboards, but rather, apple boxes stacked one on top of the other. That's where the old lady kept a lot of her stuff. They also had several nice trunks in which they stored their better things, including buckskin clothing, beadwork and their ceremonial items. My grandfather was the owner and keeper of several Medicine Bundles, including the famous Circle Dance Medicine Pipe.

"All this was during the Great Depression; back home in Canada we hardly had any money or belongings, but with my grandfather Bird Rattler's help we were able to start getting some things. He always had money and he was very kind to us, generous to everybody. All I had to say was, 'Grandfather, I want this or that,' and he would get it for me. Not big things, just little useful items. Dur-

*ing this time the people on his reservation were given
$85 each as some kind of per capita payment from the
deal with Yellowstone National Park, which used to be
part of Blackfoot country. That was a lot of money back
then, so it went a long ways. A loaf of bread was ten
cents; a pound of lard was ten cents; a dozen eggs were
ten cents; with a dollar you could buy a lot."*

*"While we were with Bird Rattler I got my first taste of
buffalo meat. The government was butchering some buffalo and they gave the meat to the Blackfeet that fall,
along with their regular rations. That was the first time I
saw an old Blackfoot delicacy we call Braided Guts. My
grandfather got hold of some buffalo intestine and he
showed me how to make this. It wasn't actually braided
but rather looped - a long piece of it - and then boiled.
It was a special treat for me to eat something my grandfather cooked, especially knowing that the last time he
ate the same thing was probably from a buffalo he killed
himself.*

*"Bird Rattler went on quite a few war raids and took sev-
eral enemy scalps during the fighting. He also captured
some famous horses from enemy camps. But his last war
raid was done after the Queen sent her Mounted Police
to forbid this, so he got put in the Fort Macleod stock-
ade. There were several of them, including your dad's
grandfather Weasel Tail (actually also a grand-uncle).
They had them in ball and chains. But the jailor felt sorry for them, so one night he left their cell door unlocked
and told them so. They took off and headed towards the
mountains, where they used a big rock to break loose
their chains. Then they made their way down to the U.S.
and settled among our southern relatives, the South Pie-
gans, where they both married and stayed for the rest of
their lives.*

*"By the time we went to stay with Bird Rattler he had al-
ready retired from being the reservation's tribal judge,
which was a very big honour. He was even taken into the*

Kiwanis club and brought to several big cities. When he died in 1937 all the stores were closed in Browning, the main town on the reservation. Later, the Kiwanis club put up a memorial for him, during which they fed about two thousand people at his old home. They also put a head stone on his grave, which was not often done back then for Indians.

Bird Rattler was highly regarded among the Blackfeet for his bravery as a warrior and buffalo hunter, and later for his work as ceremonial leader and a tribal judge. As a tribal delegate he travelled to several large cities, and was made a member of the Kiwanis Club.
Hileman Photo - Glacier Studio

"It was nice staying with my granduncle Bird Rattler, because he treated us so good. I did all their laundry and other household work, and your dad took care of his farm and horses. He couldn't ride horseback too well anymore, so daddy hooked up his team and drove him to town wherever he wanted to go, or else to visit his friends, to dances, or to ceremonies. We really got to see some of the old time Blackfoot way of life that was still going at the time.
"In Bird Rattler's home the rules were about as strict as they had been with Heavy Head and Eagle Plume. Every

*Medicine Bundle in the tribe has its own rules that have
to be followed, and that's how it was for his Circle Dance
Pipe. It was kept wrapped up with its bundle, hanging on
a wall at the back, where none of us were allowed to go.
Each spring it was opened and a lot of people danced in
a long line with different parts of it, Bird Rattler in the
lead with the medicine pipe.*

*Gets Water was the wife and
ceremonial partner of Bird
Rattler when my mom and
dad stayed with them in the
1930's, though she also
had kids from a previous
marriage. She is wearing a
typical Blackfoot dress of
buckskin decorated with
rows of beads and cowrie
shells.*
Hileman Photo - Glacier Studio

*"There was an altar in front of the bundle for making in-
cense and no one was supposed to go around it either.
But your oldest brother William was just an infant that
time and the altar was down on the floor, so it was hard
to tell him. Instead, we found out that William was scared
of this bag made out of hoofs, so Bird Rattler put it by
his altar and pointed it out, and after that he had no
more trouble.*
*"Among the frequent visitors to Bird Rattler's home was
his wife's daughter Cecile, the mother of the old man's favoured child James Boy. Her Indian name was Kills-*

Instead, given to her by an old warrior, but she was a very pleasant and fine looking lady. She made a lot of craftwork, and her beading was as good as I've ever seen. The painting on this book's cover shows her around the time we were down there, when she was married to Oscar Boy.

"If nothing further had happened we might still be living down in the States today, since Bird Rattler was going to give us some of his land; he had quite a bit of acreage along the Cutbank River. But your dad started having stomach trouble and we learned that he needed to have his appendix removed. The old man wanted him to go to the hospital in Great Falls, but from what we'd heard about Indians going there, too often just their bodies came back, so your dad decided to come up to Canada instead. He told Bird Rattler, 'If I die from my operation, at least I'll be home.' Operations were not all that perfect in those days, especially for Indians, so it seemed.

"When we got ready to go, Bird Rattler asked us to leave William with him. He already had one grandson to whom he was quite attached, but I guess he wanted another one. Daddy wouldn't hear of it. He told the old man, 'We'll return with him when I get better.'

"Bird Rattler came to town and bought us both new clothing and then a couple boxes of groceries. We didn't know he would die before we could bring William back. We left from Browning by train and went to Coutts, then north across "the line" to Lethbridge, Alberta, where we caught a bus to Cardston, on the edge of the Blood Reserve. Trouble was, this bus arrived in town during the middle of the night and we didn't have any money left for a room in the hotel. Instead, we walked uphill to the Indian hospital, where they gave daddy a bed in the men's ward and let me spend the night with the women."

I'm surprised that Bird Rattler didn't suggest for my dad to see a native doctor first, since that's probably what he himself would have done. In the 1930's there were still quite a number of them practicing among the four Blackfoot tribes, though I don't know if anyone had a remedy for appendicitis. These healers practiced fairly openly even when it was known that the government was opposed, with agents and missionaries always watching for opportunities to discredit them, or even arrest them should one of their patients die.

The three-story, red-brick Blood Indian Hospital, where I and many others of our tribe have been born - and some died - since it was opened in 1928. The photo was taken from the highway that runs along the edge of our reserve and reaches the nearby Rocky Mountains. Former Blood lands across that highway have been controlled for many years by Mormon settlers, but my parents and most others have no knowledge of such a land transaction. In the foreground stands the Catholic priest Father Leverne, for whom a small community on our reserve is now named. Although a respected and well-meaning man, he would have seen this hospital as another important step in fulfilling his church's goal to have our people leave behind natural healers, spiritual leaders and the tribal complex of ceremonies. But, like this old hospital, Blood cultural and traditional ways continue to survive into the 21st century.
Provincial Archives of Alberta Photograph Collection

Back then our Indian hospital had sort of an open-door policy for people who were stuck in town, providing them a home away

from home, where one was always sure to find friends and relatives. This was especially important in the days before telephones, welfare offices or traveller's assistance, when only a few
Indian people had cars. If someone from the reserve travelled far
away it wasn't unusual for them to sleep in a station waiting
room or on a park bench, nor did they feel as uncomfortable
about doing so as would most non-natives. It is still a common
native custom to have your visitors stay overnight, even if your
house is already well filled. Often in my young days I shared my
bed with cousins or other girls whose parents had stopped by for
the night. In the past it was part of our culture to share practically everything with visitors. Today many of us tend to be more
cautious about sharing, in part because of our church and school
influence stressing the values of "saving." Also partly because we
have learned that some people like to take advantage of those
liberal customs by always taking but seldom giving back. In the
old days people like that would have had no choice but to pitch
in, for the sake of mere survival, while today life treats us easy
and lets us exploit generous customs if we want to. It is a theme
that brings discord and confrontations in households within the
native community as well as without, another modern intrusion
for which our elders left no clear answers.

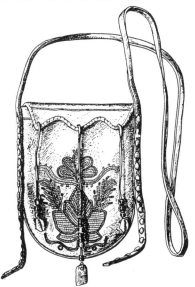

5.

Trying to Make Our Own Home

*"After your dad's operation we started staying with my
family on the reserve, although I was sure looking forward to a home of our own. My father had a crippling
disease that was getting pretty bad by this time, so we
went there to help out. Either your dad or my brother
Howard would drive my dad to town in his buggy whenever he asked them, though by that time my grandfather
Heavy Head actually owned a car, which was kept
parked outside. He was an old medicine man and of
course had no idea how to drive, but he bought himself
this big Overland sedan because he liked it. This is the
same man who prided himself on the horses that were de-
scended from those he captured long before on his war
raids. He would get your dad to be his chauffeur, or
someone else who knew how to drive. He wasn't the only
one among those old timers with a car that he couldn't
drive - a few of them liked the luxury of an automobile
but weren't interested enough to learn how to use it.*
*"In those days your dad and I took work wherever we
could find it - cutting hay, gathering sugar beets, picking
apples. During sugar beet season we could earn money
right near the reserve, where some of the big fields were.
Sometimes we brought along our tent to live in, other
times they provided us with accommodations. At one
place they gave us an empty house to live in, so we
brought our mattresses and put them on the floor, along
with our bedding. There was a cookstove and a table,
but otherwise we lived on a plain board floor, with not
even linoleum. There were two bedrooms, plus a large
living room and dining room combined. There were three*

*groups of families sharing that house. Jim Knife and his
family had one bedroom, the other was used by Rosie
Yellow Feet, and we stayed in the living room. During
the days we took our children with us out into the fields
where we worked. Finally we decided it would be easier
to leave our children behind, so one woman out of our
group was chosen to stay home with them, but we all
gave her a share of the earnings, so that everyone was
paid equal. The wife of Jim Knife was the one who
stayed, and luckily her breasts always had a lot of milk,
since she had to end up nursing everybody's babies until
we got back home from work. In between, she chopped
wood and made a big meal for all of us to share. One
time I was chosen to take care of the kids, but in the end
I never got my share of the pay, so that time is not a very
good memory for me."*

*Harvesting sugar beets was seasonal work that provided ambi-
tious Indians like my parents with a small amount of cash not
far from home, in an era when jobs were hard to find. My dad is
on the right, along with Dick Wells and his old uncle Edgar
Sitting Bull (who wears braids). At left is my grandmother
Pretty Crow Woman, who worked right alongside the men to
help support her crippled husband.*
Collection of Good Medicine Foundation

Mothers of today often wish there were alternatives to the big impersonal child care centers that many end up using; I wonder if some work places could not adapt the method used in my mother's time, of having one or another of the fellow mothers watch several kids in return for her share of the wages. Imagine a worker at a daycare centre growing so close to her charges that she'd be willing to nurse them at her own breasts, as that woman did. Actually, it has been of deep concern for many years to the women of my mother's generation that girls nowadays hardly nurse their babies anymore. They cannot understand the reason why medical doctors and nurses pushed so hard for young mothers to put their babies on formula; they consider nursing a very important bond between mother and child. Modern mothers would probably feel uncomfortable nursing someone else's child. In those times, when two children nursed together from the same woman they were considered like sisters and brothers from then on.

"We spent the winter of 1947 in a tent, since we still
didn't have our own home and wanted to be close to
where your dad worked. He had a job as ranch hand for
a man named Ryree, who lived a few miles away from the
reserve. It was a white canvas wall tent like you still see
at the Sun Dance camps or at Indian Days. Some fami-
lies lived in these until not so long ago.
"There was already snow on the ground when we went to
put this tent up, so we had to shovel a clear space first.
The rancher gave us some lumber with which to build a
floor inside of our tent. We also moved in a big cast-iron
cook stove that we bought for six dollars. We made our
beds on top of large piles of hay, which kept us up away
from the cold on the ground. I had sewn flannelette
sheets to the inside walls of our tent, just like the inner
linings of a tipi. When it got really cold, I put big pieces
of cardboard between these sheets and the tent walls
themselves. In that way we were pretty comfortable, your
dad and I, along with our five children; you and two of

your brothers were not born yet.
"We had an enjoyable Christmas that year, in spite of
our living conditions. I made a big dinner with all the
trimmings, plus cakes and pies. We also got presents for
all the kids. One thing I always enjoyed was looking at
your dad as he watched his children opening their gifts.
Since he was sort of an orphan, he never got very much
when he was small."

The chapel at St. Mary's School, where our family has often
prayed. Two nuns and a priest are in the chairs up front, while
the nativity scene at left shows that it's Christmas time. Even
our most dedicated ceremonial leaders were willing to attend
church services when asked, feeling no conflict between differ-
ent ways of addressing the Creator. Too bad the missionaries
weren't equally open-minded and receptive.
Provincial Archives of Alberta Photograph Collection

Christ was always a part of Christmas in my parents' home
and still is to this day, but our native culture was involved as well.
For one thing, we always invited some elders to join our family
for Christmas dinner. One of them would pray for all of us in
our native language, while each of us took a little piece of turkey
or whatever and held it in the air, making our own prayers at the
same time, just as we do at our traditional ceremonies. After-

wards, someone would gather up these bits of food and bring them outside, give them back to the earth as an offering, then we would start to eat.

Christmas Eve we'd go to Mass, the church being just a few miles down the country road from our family farm. But the next night we'd go to the community hall for a big pow-wow instead, where dancers dressed in tribal clothing, put on their bells and feathers, then paid honour to our native heritage. We'd meet all our friends and relatives at this pow-wow and have a happy all-night celebration.

> *"Although your dad and I learned to celebrate Christmas in the white man's way from the nuns and priests when we were young at school, we didn't use a tree at home during our early years of being married. We would take the presents for our children and just hide them wherever they couldn't be easily found. The Christmas dinner was always the main thing; even when we were really poor, we never did without one. If I couldn't afford a turkey, I'd stuff one of our big chickens instead. I also made fruitcakes and plum pudding, and from the stores in town we'd bring home mandarin oranges, nuts and candies."*

One important image I have of Christmas dinners is of my mom being so busy cooking and serving us that she never sat down to enjoy the meals herself. We'd tell her to come and sit down with us, but all she'd say is, "No, this is my day to really serve you and it makes me very happy to see all of you enjoying my cooking." Then she'd walk off claiming she was already full just from smelling all the food. My children say I learned my mother's cooking example pretty well, and that makes me glad.

> *"At one point your Aunt Emma even came to stay with us for a week, and there was still enough room in that tent for all of us. The stove worked very good, burning coal, so we were always cozy and warm. We even had some en-*

tertainment - our very first radio - which dad bought at a
second hand store in town for twelve dollars. It used a
special large battery and was one of the first radios that I
lived around. Sometimes the rancher came out near our
tent and heard it playing, then he would say, 'Oh, you
like jazz music!'

Actually, my mother doesn't care much for jazz; what she
really likes is old time country-western, and of course hymns.
But Indians in general are very music-oriented and my family
was no different. First of all, my father has always been good at
Indian songs, even winning prizes for his pow-wow singing and
drumming. We often heard that kind of music in our home, especially when older relatives came to visit, such as my dad's uncles and his brother Bernard. My father also played guitar and
taught all his boys to do the same. Sometimes they used to sing
together at concerts and at church, especially around Christmas
and at Easter. Also, when our family went on trips - after we got
a car - we would sing all kinds of songs along the way.

"Sometimes I felt sorry for your dad when he had a job
somewhere; it seemed that because he was an Indian
they often gave him the hardest work. I recall one bitterly
cold winter day when all the others were allowed to work
around the feedlot, while he was sent way out into the
fields alone to go get hay. That used to be a tough job
on icy days, especially on the way out to wherever the
hay was staked, since he had to ride on top of the open
hay rack. Coming back wasn't quite so bad, since he had
the load of hay for warmth and wind protection. He was
quite overdue getting back from this trip - we didn't
know that he had trouble along the way. That rancher
sure was glad to finally see him and after that he was
more thoughtful about sending him out into the cold all
alone. It wouldn't take long for somebody to freeze to
death when the temperature was thirty or forty below zero
and a wind was blowing as well."

If you are not an Indian with experience as a laborer, then you may not believe that my dad was actually given worse jobs than other employees, but unfortunately this happened a great many times. That's one of the reasons my parents encouraged all their children to get a good education, so they wouldn't have to do other people's lowest labors. When I was still in school I had a desire to study nursing, but when my dad found out he talked me out of it, saying, 'As an Indian they will give you all the dirtiest jobs, and that's not what I had in mind for you!' Of course, not all employers discriminated against their Indian workers; in some cases there were strong friendships formed instead.

"All this time we still had no home of our own. Then your dad got a job with the Indian Department, and when his boss found out that we had no home he told him that my grandfather Heavy Head had a lot of land, some of which had not been used by anyone for a long time. So your dad went to see Heavy Head about it and the old man agreed that we should have some - he even gave us more than we asked for. This land was near his house and the house of my parents and also not very far from your dad's family over by Bullhorn Coulee.

"Your dad went up to the mountains to cut logs for our new house. He was helped by his two favorite uncles, Willie Eagle Plume and Jack Low Horn, each of them driving a wagon. They had to make two long trips, but with that they had enough to build us a one-room log house. You and one of your brothers were born while we lived in it, so with seven children it became quite small, but still we were comfortable. We had the walls covered with plasterboard and painted; the floor was well covered with what we called 'battleship linoleum;' we also had furniture, including beds, a cupboard, a chrome table and some chairs. The children and I hauled water for the home in summer; your dad brought it up from the river with a team and sled in winter, using barrels."

My mom felt pretty much accomplished when this photo was taken in 1950. She's finally got her own log house, several nice outbuildings for her farm animals, a nice buggy to drive to town and - wrapped up in her arms - a baby girl that would grow up to write this book with her. Our family water barrel is on the right.
Collection of Good Medicine Foundation

Hauling water by hand into my homes has been a lifelong thing with me, though I didn't expect that. I still recall one of the first novelties that intrigued me when I arrived at boarding school was the indoor plumbing, especially running water. However, my husband and I took up life not long after I finished school, at which point we agreed on a simple lifestyle that has so far included the daily pumping up of fresh water, to be carried into the house.

You might think that a family of nine (plus visitors!) would crowd a one-room log house so that things would be a mess, but I can report that my mom was always a very good housekeeper. Her walls were washed four times a year, whether they needed it or not. She washed her floors every other day, usually with bath water that she saved from us kids. I was fourteen before we got electricity on the reserve (though I don't live with any of that now, either).

"We never had much money, but still we always got by. Your dad was working for the Indian Department, running a tractor where they were breaking new land to farm. He got paid every week so we managed to get groceries, in addition to the meat we received at the reserve's ration house, according to our treaty promises. Sometimes he worked there as a meat cutter, besides, so then we would get extra meat in payment, instead of money.

"To clothe my kids I often made them things like jeans. I would buy denim and take apart a pair of store-bought jeans to use for a pattern - a worn pair. I even used yellow thread, so they ended up looking almost the same. The legs were the hardest part; I soon learned that if they were not cut right they would twist. I also made shirts for the boys out of flour sacks. After the crop from our land was in, we would bring one wagon load down to the Hutterite colony where they would make it into flour for us. This flour came back in white sacks and those are the ones I used for shirts. Sometimes I even dyed this material. I also made dish towels from those sacks, and pillow cases. These I would embroider, usually by using flower transfers that were ironed on. Those are the things I learned to do from the nuns - all the girls I knew from school were handy with their work at home, making their own things, sewing for their families. To this day I feel like doing so, but in my old age it's getting hard for me.

"It sure helped the family budget that we grew our own vegetables at that time, raised some chickens for meat and eggs, even sold some of our extra products. One year I sold twenty turkeys to the priest at St. Mary's School and he really liked them for the Christmas meal. Without electricity we didn't have refrigerators, so every house had a food box somewhere on the shady side; it was either nailed to a wall of the house or buried under the ground. That's where we kept our milk, eggs, butter and meat; when I was cooking I'd have to go out there

*and get whatever I needed. Of course, we didn't keep
fresh meat for long - the good parts were quickly cut up
and hung on strings to dry, while the rest was usually
cooked by boiling or roasting. We also had salt pork,
which keeps good in any cool place.*

*"Most houses in those days had root cellars; your dad
built one by our log house. He dug a big square pit and
put a log roof over it, and that was our root cellar. It
worked good for the potatoes from our garden, also the
carrots and turnips, which we covered with some dirt to
help them keep better. We hung our onions on the root
cellar walls and when we needed anything from there we
made a trip outside to get it. We even put my canning
down there, because one or another of you kids were always opening the jars if we stored them at the house.
Some people even had their root cellars right under the
wooden floors of their houses. It wasn't till later that we
started having refrigerators."*

Eating habits in our tribe made a radical change when electric
power brought refrigerators into our lives. The change has been
almost as radical as the earlier one of going from a buffalo-
dependant lifestyle to the reservation and government food. Education has only recently been getting across the message to reserve youngsters that there's a lot of unhealthy stuff taking over
their diets, stuff we don't know anything about. My mother may
have cooked more like an ordinary ranch wife than like an old
time Blood Indian, but she still depended on food raised mainly
near her own home, whereas now we don't even know the places
that much of our food comes from.

*"Among the things that I canned each year were wild
berries, though in my grandmother's time these were always just dried. A group of us women would go berry
picking together, including my mother and my brother's
wife Mabel, then afterwards I'd take my share and can it
in jars. I used to end up with thirty quarts or more of*

Saskatoons. Later in the summer when chokecherries got ripe, we'd gather these and I'd use some for making syrup. But I also crushed a bunch in the same way as my grandmother did, mixing them with meat and rendered fat to make our traditional pemmican. Often I would send pemmican to work with your dad - for his lunch - just like my grandmother did for her husband when he went off hunting, or on a war trail."

"You are what you eat" is a popular expression nowadays, but it also describes the attitude of our people towards food. For instance, the decline of our tribal culture is traced back to our loss of the buffalo, since everything in our life was focused on this animal and we gave it special sacred status because of that. Sure we still give thanks for having pork and beans, or rice, but they have no religious significance for us otherwise.

"Sometimes I think about the food nowadays that comes from far away. I think about the ships that have to travel from other lands in order to bring us this food, and each of them leaves behind its own trail of pollution. Then I recall how my grandfather Heavy Head told us children that we are not used to that kind of food and that it would make us sick. So I believe that a lot of the sicknesses we now suffer are caused by what we eat.

"It's sad to witness our young people being so much like non-natives that they hardly eat any natural food. It seems they'd rather eat fast food just to stay up with their crowd. One of my adopted daughters cooks for the students at school; she makes stews, chilies, salads and other healthy things, and she bakes their bread, but she says that a lot of them turn their noses up at her meals and wait until they can drive to town for a quick hamburger or other junk food. The only hope is that we can educate the future generations better right from the start, so they'll know what healthy food is."

We ate healthy in my mom's household when I was young - she always had a big vegetable garden, plus chickens, ducks, geese and pigs. By that time the government had finally succeeded in getting the wild and nomadic Blackfeet to turn into farmers on their own lands. But then lo and behold, they changed their minds (and policies) on us. New bureaucrats in the 50's and 60's came and said - in effect - 'these Indian lands would make a lot more money through modern ranching techniques than by these old fashioned family homestead methods.' So they quit providing us with farm tools and equipment - tractors and such - and put all their efforts into talking us out of working our own land.

Blood Indians - horsemen of the Northern Plains - learning to use horses in a new way. In this case, several Blood ranchers have brought their teams to plow a farm for the new St. Paul's Anglican Residential School, not far from St. Mary's on the Blood Reserve. Indian farmers often preferred working with horses rather than tractors for cultural reasons, though government bureaucrats just saw that as more proof that they were inefficient.
Collection of Glenbow Archives

Modern ranching skills were not well known among our people, so we were persuaded to lease most of our reserve - the biggest one in Canada - to non-natives. Sure enough, they produced a lot more than we ever did, paying us a share of the profits, which at first looked like a bonanza to us, even though they kept the greater share for themselves. But in the end, it again made us dependent on somebody else for money, and worst of all it took away a major family focus. Instead of working together every day to make our living, which had at least some similarity to life in the buffalo days, we now waited for an annual check that was often bigger than we knew how to spend properly all at one time.

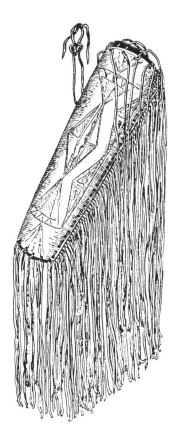

6.

Calling on the Medicine Men and Women

Traditional healing among our people depended first and foremost on the power of prayer. Whatever herbs and rituals were used by the individual medicine man and woman, prayer always came first. Prayers accompanied the preparation of herbal remedies, their administration, even their gathering. For this reason the missionaries put a lot of effort into opposing and discrediting our healers, saying theirs was "the devil's work" and so on. While their negative efforts had only limited effects on the older people of our tribe - even those in my mom's generation - it worked so well on us younger folks that we grew up with our minds pretty well closed to such natural ways of healing. We were afraid of our own medicine men and women, not wanting to get near anything to do with the "devil."

Although my mom otherwise accepted much of what the missionaries taught and has been a lifelong follower of the Catholic church, she didn't buy the devil story about our healers, preferring their remedies whenever possible - even for her own children - often having less faith in the white doctors than in those of our own tribe. She witnessed the powers of our natural methods while growing up around her grandparents, especially old Heavy Head who was considered a leading doctor with numerous successful cures to his credit.

> *"Three of your brothers had health problems when they were young, especially Leroy. At that time we still travelled mostly with horses and wagons, so it was quite a trip to go into town for a doctor or the hospital. As a result, I sometimes relied on our old Indian doctors to help out with family ailments. At one point Leroy was so sick that I got a whole bunch of medicine men and women to-*

gether at the same time. They sure did work hard to treat him in their traditional ways.

"At this time in his life your brother was having convulsions that made him so sick that he was just about paralyzed. He couldn't swallow, he couldn't eat, and he had a hard time in the bathroom. I went through a lot of anxiety over all this, so that's why I got these Indian doctors to come and see if they could help out.

"In a way it was like having a pow-wow dance in our house, with people sitting all around, visiting, singing, praying and eating. There was a bed for your brother in the middle, with my mother Pretty Woman sitting on one side and my grandmother White Shield Woman on the other. They were the ones taking care of him in between the actual doctoring. I had a baby at this time, so I sat across the room and looked after it. My father was there too, but he just sat and stared at my boy; we had a picture of the Virgin Mary by his head and my father was praying to that for help.

"For ten days and ten nights they doctored him, working on him straight through. Among these doctors was Chris Bull Shields, Brown Chief Calf, and a very old man named Not Good, who was also the keeper of a Beaver Medicine bundle. Of course, my grandfather Heavy Head helped with the doctoring, as did an old lady named Brass Woman, the wife of White Man Left. She was the only woman among those who were doing the actual healing; she had her own powers for that. Thus they all took turns, doctoring him day and night.

"Whenever they were going to call on their healing powers they would first put earth paint on him; they would use that same paint and put some of it on themselves. This is common at the start of all kinds of Blackfoot ceremonies, not only those used for healing.

"Some of them needed hot rocks for part of their healing procedure. We would heat these rocks for them in our stove. They'd put the hot rocks into a dish of water and

*from that they would spray some of this water on the pa-
tient, using a hollow bird bone of some kind, most often
eagle. Usually they'd have some of their special roots or
herbs in their mouths, which they'd chew up and mix
with the water spray. These medicine people didn't say in
our language that they were doctoring; their expression
was, "We will take care of him." That's what they said
about your brother Leroy, and they did.*

*"We fed them three meals a day during the ten days that
they were here. They brought their own bedrolls and took
turns at naps whenever they could. Sometimes they
stayed up all night. If they thought he was not doing
good they'd jump up right then and start to doctor. If we
noticed that he was getting worse we'd tell them right
away, asking them to take care of him.*

*"They each sang their power songs for doctoring when it
was their turn to work on him. Sometimes your dad and
your uncle Howard drummed for them. They did the
singing and doctoring, but they always got someone else
to beat the drums.*

*"We paid them in money, horses, goods and whatever
else we could. My cousin Alfred Sweetgrass helped us by
contributing a cow with which to feed the people while
they were at our house and for them to have some meat
to bring home when they left. My brother Howard helped
out too. That's the way these things were done. Each one
got ten dollars cash; some got horses, and we gave out
shirts, blankets and things; my grandmother gave Brass
Woman a nice shawl.*

*"Other relatives helped us too. This took place in the
middle of winter and the snow was quite deep. People
would come by to check on things, to bring us wood for
the stove and to give a little something in support. In
those days word got around quickly, and we all helped
each other wherever we could.*

*"Some of these old time Indian doctors had special ways
that they used to check if their patient was going to re-*

*cover. For instance, Brass Woman had a little stick figure
that she set up by Leroy while she was doctoring. She
kept blowing on it while she worked. We already knew
that if it fell over she would consider this a bad omen, a
sign that she couldn't help him. It stayed upright the
whole time.*

*"Chris Bull Shields had a different way to make his test.
He started singing his power songs and while he was
singing them really hard he suddenly started to tickle my
boy. Leroy jumped right up, so old Chris told him, 'Come
to me.' Leroy walked to him as if nothing was wrong, so
the old man said, 'He will get better now.' To this day
Leroy is still up and going about his life, working as a
university professor, using his legal studies, and even
hosting a radio talk show. You would not have thought
he could make it if you had seen him so sick. He was
doctored for everything important during those ten days
and nights - for sleeping, eating, passing water, even
how to walk. It was like starting life over again, and then
he got better. All these prayers said for him have really
helped him in life, that is my belief."*

Although I said earlier that my generation grew up not thinking much about this traditional form of healing, I'm happy to
tell you that it nevertheless survived and has seen a tremendous
revival in the last decade or so. Not only that, but a lot of the new
Indian doctors have the advantage of modern education to
broaden their knowledge of plants and cures, though very few
understand the many spiritual powers those old time buffalo
healers had.

The survival of our native healing ways is largely because
those of my mother's generation still had enough faith to bring
their own children for treatments, as she has just described, there-
by giving us experiences that counterbalanced what we were told
in school and church. It says a lot to me that my mother kept up
this strong faith in our own ways even while she held the church
in such high regard as well.

Of course, there were some non-natives who also supported our ways of doctoring, even people in the outside medical community. I recall one of my nieces being in the hospital, so sick that the doctors there were quite worried. A well liked old woman named Mrs. Mountain Horse, or Homeward Offering as she was called in our language, was allowed to give my niece one of her herbal brews. For just five minutes they were alone together, and after that my niece felt better and improved.

An interesting example of respect between the two ways of doctoring took place in the early 70's and involved Willie Scraping White, or Wolf Old Man, one of the last old time healers and ceremonial leaders, a proud man in his 90's, who used to visit my husband and I in order to teach us some of his traditions. He would only attempt to treat ailments with which he was familiar, saying there are many new ones for which natural remedies are not enough. Whether for friends or for himself, he said such ailments should be treated by medical doctors. So he kept in his doctoring suitcase not only little pouches and bags filled with plants he'd gathered, but also the drugstore prescriptions from his good friend, the doctor in town. This man took old Willie for his first flight at age 93, in his own private plane, thus sharing an event of spiritual significance with his fellow doctor.

> *"There was another time that your brother also got sick and the memory of the doctoring on that occasion now makes me laugh, though at the time we were pretty worried. I had been home alone with him, while we were living in the log house next door to my grandparents. He started going into spasms, so I quickly wrapped him up in a blanket and rushed him over to the old folks, since they were good at doctoring.*
> *"Someone had told me that when he got those convulsions I should put him into lukewarm mustard water. I was willing to try any remedy, so I kept some of it on hand, but when the time came I was too excited so I just ran out. By this time he was unconscious, so I handed him to my grandparents and told them to take care of*

him, while I rushed back for the dish of water.

"When I returned with it, the old folks were singing away - my grandmother was beating on a rawhide drum and my grandfather Heavy Head was going through his doctoring motions. He had his eyes closed. I just rushed up, grabbed Leroy by the ankles and dunked him into the water. He cried out, which really surprised the old folks because it came from a different direction than where they had put him. Their eyes had been closed when I took him, so for a moment they looked quite puzzled.

My mom's grandfather Heavy Head, also called White Elk, in his final years, around the time he did the doctoring in her story.
Collection of Glenbow Archives

"Those Indian doctors had supernatural powers, they didn't just heal people in the ordinary way. They were very private with those powers - they kept them secret. They always had them along, but they usually wouldn't talk about them. If someone gets power, they won't broadcast it, they'll just keep it to themselves. Then too, they're not sure at first if it will really happen, if the pow-

er will work, so they wait and test themselves first.

"The song is really important; their power comes when the song is sung. If a doctor has a wife, he will teach the song to her so that she can sing it with him. When he is asked to do any doctoring, if his wife is present, she has to sit close to him and sing along. That makes the healing ceremony all the more powerful.

"A person who has the power to doctor will not volunteer himself or herself to the patient. At the most, he might tell a friend, 'That one over there is sick, why don't you go tell him to come here to me?' The person that wants to hire a medicine man or woman will take along some kind of gift to present them with the request. He'll say, 'Here is a present for you. I'm relying on you. So and so is very sick, come and take care of them for me.' That's the proper way to hire an Indian doctor's services. The doctor will go right away; he won't wait if he knows the person is sick.

"When the doctor gets to the sick person, he starts out by painting the patient's face with sacred earth, usually red or yellow, then he'll paint himself. After that he'll spread out his doctoring stuff - his herbs and tools and sacred items. He doesn't keep them hidden; whoever is there can see them. Then he calls for a basin of water to be brought, and a hot rock which has been heating in the fire. When the rock is white hot, then he knows it is ready.

"The rock is brought to the medicine man on a shovel and put into the basin, causing the water to boil. At that point the doctor will sing his song to bring on his power - to bring in the spirit thing that will help him in healing. Then he'll have the power to do supernatural things, things that I've seen so I know that they're true.

"For instance, one will pick up the hot rock in his hand without getting burned and he'll use that power for healing. Or he'll drink some of the boiling water. He'll be chewing his special herbs all this time and these he will mix with the water that he sprays on the sick person, es-

*pecially on the place where they are ailing, he concen-
trates all those powers on that place.*

*"Some doctors got their power from certain birds or ani-
mals and they would bring along these skins to represent
them. When their power came, these skins were sometimes
seen to get up and move around, helping with the doctoring. My father once saw a man who was badly shot,
getting cured by an Indian doctor and a pair of water
birds, which represented his power. He saw them at first
just as feathers and dried skins, but then they got up and
danced around the fireplace while the doctor sang. That
man was almost dead, but when those birds jumped up
on his body and danced around on his wound, he started moving, and then slowly he regained consciousness.
By the time they went back to being just skins and feathers he had opened his eyes and asked for something to
eat. Later he was doctored the same way again, then after that he recovered completely.*

*"There were quite a few women who doctored, as well as
men. One of them that was often talked about when I was
young was Beaver Woman, though she lived before my
time. There were lots of stories about how powerful she
was and the lives that she saved. Chris Bull Shields went
to where she was buried and slept there, so she gave him
some of her power in his dreams. That's what he used to
doctor your brother Leroy. He became a very popular
doctor because of her.*

*"These doctors usually specialized in certain ailments,
but they would heal men and women alike. For instance,
my old grandmother First to Kill had something wrong
with her liver; in Indian we say 'she was being beaten.'
She would get really sick with it, so sick that she'd pass
out. My grandfather Heavy Head doctored her for it, but
she was still getting sicker so they sent for an older doctor named Gets Wood at Night, whose other name was
Calf Coming over the Hill. He was a relative of the family, so somebody went to get him in a wagon.*

*He arrived that evening; it was dark already. We had
everything prepared for him. In those days we kept a special pile of rocks on hand that we gathered according to
instructions. Those doctors couldn't just use any kind of
rock; for instance, they wouldn't use the ones that have
sparkles in them because they will crack in the heat. Also,
they just want smooth rocks.*

"*Gets Wood at Night picked a rock from our pile that he
liked and we heated it for him. We were also cooking for
everyone who was there; it was another time that we had
several doctors to help out.*

"*Finally the rock he had selected was hot and ready so
he opened his special medicine bag and took out his
power shirt - a canvas garment with holes cut out all
over it - and he put this on. He did this according to directions he received in his dreams, though it would have
been improper for anyone to ask him about the details.
We brought the hot rock and basin of water to him, at
which point an old lady who was visiting said, 'I will put
the rock in - I've been suffering from a sore shoulder.'
By helping with the doctoring work in that way she expected to get relief from her pain.*

"*Gets Wood at Night then told my grandmother, 'You
will put your head towards the door, so that when I finish
doctoring you with this rock you can throw it outside.'
The bad part of the ailment was considered to be in that
rock afterwards, which is why he wanted her to throw it
out. During the actual doctoring he always told us to
keep the door closed. There were several reasons for this,
one of them being to keep dogs out. Most medicine men
and women felt that dogs would distract their powers and
keep them from properly working.*

"*So then they started singing; he had several drummers
all sitting in a row. Two of them were John Day Chief
and Nelson Rabbit. Another one was Willie Scraping
White, although he was doctoring her at the same time.
Your dad sat on the wood pile by the door, ready to feed*

the fire and perform whatever other work was needed.
"While that old medicine man was singing, a couple of
the women took the hot rock out with a big spoon and
brought it to him. He kept on with the song, moving his
body in time to its rhythm, rubbing himself on different
parts of his body.
"Finally in the midst of his singing and praying he sud-
denly said, 'Okeeh,' which meant he was ready for the
next stage, so they put the' red hot rock into his hands.
He took it and was sort of snorting, then he started roll-
ing it around on his chest - four times - before he finally
put it back into the water.
"Then he took out his bird bone tube and started spray-
ing her with the hot water. When he got finished with this
part he asked for the door to be opened so that she could
throw the rock out. As it flew through the door, your dad
ducked so quickly that he nearly fell off his perch on the
woodpile. He told me later that it looked like it was com-
ing right at him. Those old people sure laughed and
thought it was funny.
"The next day Gets Wood at Night doctored my grand-
mother again. This time instead of a basin he used the
skull of some animal that must have helped him with its
power. He asked my mother to boil some water, which he
poured into this skull cup, then he added four pieces of
special grass, one at each of the four directions. Finally
he put in a teaspoon of his special herbal mixture, which
was already crushed. He allowed this to steep in the hot
water for a while, then he made my grandmother sit up
and he told her, 'Here, drink this - you will drink every-
thing, plants and all.' He swished it around a bit and
then told her to drink it down quickly. When she was fin-
ished he said, 'There, for as long as you live you will
have no more trouble with your liver. I'm an old man
and I'm the only one left who can take care of this for
you.' And he was right - we never had to worry about
her with this ailment again."

My mother said Gets Wood at Night died not long after this and that he was right in saying, 'I'm the last one who can do this for you.' Although some of his power later came to her own grandfather Heavy Head through dreams, and he was a noted doctor in his own right, none of the medicine men and women since his time were so capable of demonstrating their mysterious powers, performing what non-believers might call magic feats.

On the other hand, considering the strong efforts by missionaries and government agents to bring our traditional ways to an end, Gets Wood at Night and other old time doctors would probably be quite surprised that here in the 1990's such healing methods are again on the rise, with several practitioners right in our own tribe. These people still combine various plants with songs and prayers, though usually not with the more esoteric performances seen in my mother's time. The basic concept here is healing by faith, and a lot of our people haven't lost that faith yet.

"I'll tell you about another time that I saw the healing powers of Gets Wood at Night, though then I was still just a child, not long after the first world war. My father was suddenly stricken with an inability to walk, and he was naturally very upset about this. Our neighbor was an old timer named Red Leggings who, although not actually a relative of ours, was very fond of our family and treated me like his own granddaughter. When he learned about my father's problem he immediately went to Gets Wood at Night and gave him a good horse to come and share his powers. Red Leggings was known for his nice herd of horses.

"For my father, Gets Wood at Night used a much different treatment than he did later for my grandmother. To begin with, he just prayed and prayed, now and then looking at my father's legs. We are believers in the power of prayer, so that alone had a strong effect on my dad.

"Eventually he took out of his medicine kit the skin of a brown weasel, which was one of his main powers. He laid

*that skin on one of my father's legs, its head pointing
down and away from my dad's head. He tied it there with
a strip of buckskin, then he made a trail for it with yellow
earth paint, leading down to my dad's shin. He made
this trail with little yellow marks that looked similar to the
tracks of weasels when they go around. Weasels have always been very special animals in our Blackfoot culture.
"At that point Gets Wood at Night told my mother, 'I'm
going next door to visit my brother-in-law Heavy Head;
I'll be back in a little while. If there is any movement,
don't lift the blanket that I used to cover his legs; don't
try to see what is happening.'
But my father was too inquisitive; after a while he told
my mother, 'Look under there and see what is going on;
I feel something moving around.' My mom tried to tell
him that he wasn't supposed to look, but he insisted, so
she pulled the blanket back just a little ways. Well, the
thong was still in place where it had been tied, but that
brown weasel skin had moved all the way down his leg to
his shin. My father was very surprised because he was not
much of a believer in supernatural things.
"In church and school they made us think these things
were evil, the devil's work, and that's why most of our
old time doctoring and healing died out. There are still
some Indian doctors working today, but they are different from these old people that I witnessed. For one thing,
they don't seem to have the same supernatural powers.
That has changed, just like everything else in our life."*

On this occasion my grandfather Joe Beebe admitted that his
doubts were proven wrong - I've even seen it in writing, since he
kept kind of a journal of interesting tales and experiences such
as this one. But for my mother to have grown up around his
doubts and then to hear these old ways outright condemned all
through her years in school, it's amazing that she continued to
have so much faith in them. The same is true for the rest of her
generation, most of whom have called on medicine men and

women to help their own children and families at various times, as my mother did for my brother. Here is another doctoring memory from her younger days in the 1920's.

"One time I had a very bad toothache, maybe an abscess. Since we lived far from town, my dad decided to have me doctored in the Indian way. Although he was a strong doubter, the other side of him leaned towards having faith in our natural methods. It so happened that at this time we had a visit from his special friend Ralph Hoof - they would say to each other 'Ni-duck-ah,' which was like being brothers - and this man had some doctoring abilities.

"Ralph Hoof's Indian name was Stretches His Leg, and I still remember telling my father in Indian, 'Ki-duck-ah Stretches His Leg has come.' I went outside to greet them and to watch how fast they put up their canvas wall tent. In those days visitors often stayed and camped for awhile, especially if they came by horse from some other part of the reserve.

"When Stretches His Leg came into our house my father told me to cook a meal for him. His wife was still outside getting beds and other things set up in their tent. My father and his close friend were glad to see each other; they talked while the man ate.

"When he finished eating, my father told his friend, 'Can you treat our daughter's painful tooth while you are here?' They thought of each other's children like their own; I considered them both my fathers, and he always called me daughter. In addition, his wife was a close relative of my grandparents.

"Requests like my father made are not turned down, especially not between close friends. So the first thing he did was fill a cup about a quarter way with tea, into which he stirred a bunch of salt. He told me to take a mouthful of this and then to tilt my head back with it so it would go on my tooth. He said, 'Don't use too much of

this, for it is very strong. While you do that I will go out to my camp and get my other medicine.' This meant his bag of herbs and plants, which these kinds of people always took with them when they travelled.

"Just two mouthfuls of that mixture were enough to make the pain go away, but my face was still all swelled up; I had a large cheek. Then he came back with a special cup of his - a very small one - inside of which I heard something rattling around which turned out to be his medicine. I didn't really know what to expect.

"Stretches His Leg told me to come and sit by him - we were both on chairs - and then he started to pray. While he was praying he took the thing that I'd heard inside of the cup - some kind of rock that represented his power - and he made me tilt my head so that he could roll that rock all around the place where the swelling was. He prayed the whole time while he did this.

"When he was finished he told me to wash my tooth with what was left of that strong tea. He performed this ritual just once, but by the next day the pain was gone and the swelling was way down. The mixture was so strong that eventually my tooth just sort of decayed away; it never did bother me again."

The nuns at the boarding school where my mom went would have been aghast to hear that one of their girls was being healed with a simple drink, plus faith in the intervening powers represented by a stone. Yet she says it definitely cured her problem, which is all she asked for. To this day she still prefers natural remedies to store bought pills and we have a heck of a time getting her to see an actual doctor when we think she might have something serious.

Incidentally, feeding and welcoming visitors to our homes is an important tribal custom that has also continued right up to today. No matter what the hour of their arrival or the number in their party, visitors to my mother's house have always been fed and offered a place to sleep. I've been in tipis at pow-wows where the hosting families had so many visitors that the floor was completely filled and left no room for walking. This is much different from the general non-native custom of phoning ahead and making special arrangements before getting together or sharing a meal, although nowadays some of our younger people have jobs and other obligations so they are following non-native ways regarding such issues as guests.

My mom and I share a laugh in the autumn of her 78th year, standing outside her house on the land where she was raised, and where she raised me.
Adolf Hungry Wolf Photo

7.

A Missionary Who Really Cared

Nurse Jane Megarry was well known on the Blood Reserve back in my mom's young days, although she spent most of her time at the St. Paul's Anglican Residential School which was located somewhat away from the mainstream, at one corner of the reserve. She was so popular with her students that stories about her are still told to this day, although it's been many years since she moved on. I never met her myself, but it was easy to get a sense of her dedication and exuberance by reading through her notebooks in the Anglican Church Archives. She truly seemed to enjoy her work at this school and with the Blood Indian kids, which is more than can be said about many of the missionaries who worked amongst us. She made extra efforts to put fun into the lives of her students back in a time when reserve schools were basically so strict and unfriendly that Indian kids were often sad.

Nurse Megarry had the foresight to realize that native children were going through difficult and important changes, so she tried to give them the best guidance she could. I've heard some of her former students say she was like a second mother through their growing up days. She herself had been raised in England and was quite familiar with the trials and tribulations of boarding school life, so she made special efforts to give her students a wide variety of interests, with the main focus always being their preparation for adulthood as farmers and ranchers. For instance, she introduced first aid training to her classrooms and made sure every student learned some of it. All her girls graduated with skills in home nursing, which was helpful on our vast prairie lands in those days before Indian families had telephones or automobiles. She taught the girls to give bed baths for the sick, to take temperatures, pulse and respiration, prepare their meals, and make them comfortable.

One result of her guidance and training was that girl students from St. Paul's school were known for asserting themselves in ways not seen before, Blackfoot society being traditionally very male dominated. Of course, some people in the tribe were not pleased by this social development and felt uncomfortable hearing young women speaking their minds. Critics said it was just a natural result of being around the superior attitude of the British. By comparison, the girls who were schooled by the more French-oriented Catholics seemed somewhat subservient.

Rivalry between Anglican and Catholic students on the reserve was common since before my mother's time and lasted through the early years of my own schooling, until the 1960's, when the federal government revised native education and curtailed direct church influence upon it. This rivalry was generally of a friendly nature among the students - even though aspects of it carried on right through adulthood - but for church authorities the rivalry was quite serious and sometimes turned bitter. For instance, government funding depended on the number of students that were enrolled, so there was a constant struggle to persuade parents into favoring one church or the other. Fortunately, Nurse Megarry appears to have concentrated her energies on helping the Indian children, not using them for political and financial gain. Here are some excerpts from the notebooks she kept.

> *"After resigning from the Galt Hospital in Lethbridge, I was appointed Nurse and Head Matron of St. Paul's Residential School on the Blood Indian Reserve, five miles from the Mormon town of Cardston, Alberta, in the foothills and fifty miles from the Majestic Rocky Mountains.*
> *"The old St. Paul's School was situated in a very picturesque place about seven miles from the old Fort Macleod and was not on the reserve as the new school was. I visited at the old school for about two months, before going on duty in the new school as that building was not completed. The old school was in rather a broken down condition and getting much too small.....*

The lady in white - Nurse Jane Megarry - on the steps of St. Paul's School with some of her pupils, about 1927. Clockwise from lower left: Olive Davis, Violet Creighton, Bella Healy and Jennie Healy.
Collection of Glenbow Archives

"At this time the Indian people were passing through the transition stage from their own way of living to the white man's way. They were not getting proper food or sufficient clothing.

"The morning of my departure from the old school was a very cold one, deep snow and temperature forty below zero. On the party....was the Rev. Canon Middleton, Principal; two Indian girls, Josephine Davis and Rosie Sleeping Woman; and myself. Ernest Iron Pipe was the driver. The wagon was drawn by four horses. We had a drive of forty miles across the open prairies.....we climbed out of the wagon at intervals and ran, to keep ourselves warm and also to make the pulling easier for the horses.

"It was after sunset when we arrived at the new school. We were all very tired, cold and hungry. When we first caught sight of the new school with the majestic Rocky

*Mountains covered with snow and ice in the distance and
the evening sun setting on them, the scene that met our
eyes was one of rugged and wild grandeur and the new
school looked like a beautiful big castle in the lovely setting of the foothills....*

*"....Through the main hall and corridors it made us feel
as if we were travelling through the hall and rooms of
some great seat of learning."*

At this point in Nurse Megarry's journal she gives a long de-
scription of the various parts that made up this new school, a
most conspicuous feature being that everything was designed to
separate the boys and girls, from dormitories and washrooms to
playrooms, hospital wards (with four beds each) and the tables in
the dining room. She doesn't actually express any concern
about boys and girls getting together (and believe me they tried,
sometimes successfully). In those days there just wasn't the kind
of mixing that we accept so commonly today.

Perhaps I should mention here that in quoting from this
lady's papers I've had to make quite a number of grammar and
spelling corrections; makes me wonder how she'd feel about
that. She capitalized words helter skelter, yet seldom did so with
the first word of a new sentence or paragraph. She invariably
wrote the word we as "Wee," and she must have thought the
supply of commas and periods was limited, as she seldom used
them when she should have. For instance, here's a paragraph just
as she wrote it.

*"There Was a Seperate Bake Room With a Large Bake
oven Where two and three Hundred White and Brown
Loaves of Bread was Baked daily and Hundreds of Currant Buns and Cake the Pies Were Baked in the Kitchen
Sunday Was the only day no Baking was done"*

One interesting aspect in the operation of this particular
school - or perhaps all boarding schools run by the Anglican
church, though I'm not familiar with them - was that they had a

"Women's Auxiliary" whose members supplied clothing and bedding for all the students, sewing individual patchwork quilts that must have given the dormitory a much homier look than most boarding schools where every bed looked just the same. The exact number of students at this school was not mentioned, but she did say there were 150 beds for them, plus twelve beds in the hospital wing and twenty beds for the staff. To this she adds, "the Boys and Girls made their own Beds Each morning the Boys Could make their Beds Just as nice as the Girls....."

Here are some further edited excerpts.

> *"The milk was brought in from the cow barns night and morning.... what the pupils used for drinking and for their porridge was not separated; they were given the whole milk as they required plenty of milk and butter, which was made three times a week in the dairy.....*
>
> *"There was a room on the main floor where the parents of the pupils could see their children when they came to visit them. There was an armory and band room also on the main floor where the musical instruments and uniforms were kept, as St. Paul's school boys had a good Cadet Corps and Band. There was also a piano, radio and gramophone. The pupils heard their music and singing lessons and practiced there. The radio was presented to the school by......then Prime Minister of Canada, afterward Lord Bennett, of Calgary.*
>
> *"The first mattresses we had in the new school for the pupils were filled with straw. I asked specifically for these for health conditions. Each summer they were emptied and washed and refilled with fresh straw. Some years later when the pupil's health improved, Indian Affairs at Ottawa sent ordinary mattresses.*
>
> *"The pupils were very much excited when they arrived at the new school. Everything now was so very strange and new.... In the old school, as in their own lodges, they had been used to lamps and candles; with wood and coal burned in stoves; water was heated for their baths in*

*large pots on top of the stoves; all the water was pumped
from the wells and carried in pails.*

*"Now everything was changed. There was bright electric
lights in all the rooms, nice warm bathrooms with show-
ers, hot and cold running water. The new beds with mattresses filled with nice fresh straw looked so very high to
them at first they were afraid they would fall out in the
night....*

*"For the first few days the pupils kept running around
the corridors and up and down the stairs, turning on water, drinking at the fountains and flashing on the electric
lights. After a few weeks they all got settled down to life
and routine at the new school and there was no damage
done to the furniture nor writing or drawing on the
walls."*

*Blood students of the 1920's pose proudly with a stack of mat-
tresses they've just filled with fresh straw.*
Collection of Glenbow Archives

To give her students something special to look forward to at
various times of the year, Nurse Megarry made sure the principal
holidays were festively observed. Christmas, New Year's and
Easter were celebrated with dinners to which the parents were in-

vited. For Halloween the students made their own costumes and competed for prizes, with the matronly nurse herself dressing up as a witch and leading them all on a spooky procession through the darkened school and down into the boiler room.

> *"As Christmas day was a very busy time at St. Paul's School with all the church services and all our visitors, Indian and white, the pupils were given their Christmas dinner on December 22nd.*
>
> *"The tables were all decorated with the school colors -- red and green -- and green shades on the electric lights, all done by the senior girls. A large Christmas cake on each table, decorated with pink and white icing, and dishes of sweets and nuts....*
>
> *"When the pupils had finished dinner, Santa Claus walked into the dining room with bells tinkling and spoke a few words of merry greetings and said he hoped to return and visit again on Christmas Eve. He then left the room amid loud cheers and clapping of many hands.*
>
> *"At midnight on Christmas Eve, Santa Claus returned to the school and went through all the dormitories filling the stockings and socks hanging from the foot of the bed of each boy and girl with oranges, sweets and toys.*
>
> *"About 10 a.m. on Christmas morning the Indian men, women and children from different parts of the Blood Reserve began to arrive for the service.....The lovely little church was usually crowded.....When the service was finished the parents came over to the school dining room and were given Christmas dinner. After dinner the parents left taking with them their children for a few days holiday.*
>
> *"After the pupils and their parents had departed, the school was very quiet - no laughter or noise of many feet running to and fro through the halls ... the great dining room was like a banquet hall, deserted.*
>
> *"The members of the school staff and our friends dined at 7 p.m. on Christmas night. After dinner we all went to*

*the music room; some played a favorite piece of music on
the piano, or sang a favorite song; others told stories of
things that happened in bygone days.*

*"After spending a week at the homes of their parents, the
pupils returned to school on New Year's eve and at 7
p.m. the members of the school staff, with the pupils and
their parents, went to the parish hall where a very large
Christmas tree was beautifully decorated with coloured
lights and shining silver icicles, bells and stars; also with
many presents which were sent to the school from different branches of the Women's Auxiliary to the Anglican
church. There were many lovely and useful gifts - hockey
sticks, gloves, scarfs, balls, books and games for the
boys; for the senior girls many necklaces of beads, warm
scarves and other useful articles of clothing; for the jun-
ior girls, many lovely dolls of all kinds and sizes.*

*"The parents were all invited to the Christmas tree party
and everyone present received a gift of some kind. Santa
Claus greeted us all in his usual merry way, then started
to distribute the gifts...there was much fun and laughter.*

*"At 11 p.m. the Indians and white people on the reserve
began to arrive at St. Paul's church for the Watch Night
service. Some of them had to travel many miles from different parts of the reserve in sleighs and wagons. At
11:30 the service started for thanksgiving to Almighty
God for the many mercies He had so graciously bestowed
and so we all said goodby to the old year.*

*"A few minutes after the dawn of the new year, we all
slowly approached the altar of the Lord on bended knees
and received the holy communion. Then everyone came
to the school dining room where currant buns, tea and
coffee were served. After wishing each other a happy new
year, our guests all left; it was usually about 3:30 on
New Year's morning....*

*"During the winter months we arranged social parties
once a month in the Parish hall for the married ex-pupils
living on the reserve. Some nights we had a fancy-dress*

> *ball, or a basket social, and some nights a picture show,*
> *as we had our own moving picture machine."*

From her childhood in England, Nurse Megarry was left with profound admiration for any kind of nobility, so she managed to involve her school kids several times in the visits by such dignitaries as "His Excellency Lord Tweedsmuir, Governor-General of Canada," who came to St. Paul's School. The school's cadet corps formed a guard of honor, while the boy's band played the national anthem. The kids were given a taste of native pride as well, when Lord Tweedsmuir stood before them in the school auditorium and received an eagle feather head dress from their old chief, Shot-on-Both-Sides, who also gave him the Indian name Eagle Face, making him an "honorary chief." The Lord said that being an Indian chief had been his dream since boyhood.

Little warriors of the Blood Reserve. Edward, Prince of Wales, inspects the cadets of St. Paul's Anglican School during a visit to Canada in the 1920's.
Collection of Glenbow Archives

But in the spring of 1937 came an opportunity for a special visit that Nurse Megarry was really proud about, taking up over twenty pages of her journal for the glowing details. It started with an invitation from Buckingham Palace for "one Indian girl" from the school to attend the coronation of King George the Sixth and

Queen Elizabeth. Although the nurse herself wasn't going, her enthusiasm for the girl was just as great. She even endured a brief challenge by the old head chief, as she was determined to send the girl while he wanted a boy. In our traditions it was unheard of to send a girl as the tribe's delegate to a major chief's conference. This event is no doubt a historical cornerstone in the social history of Blackfoot women. It was also of great inspiration for the girl who experienced it, as she went on to find much respect in her life. Here are some edited excerpts about it taken from Nurse Megarry's longhand.

Girl Guides exercise in front of the girl's dormitory at St. Paul's School in the 1920's. Blackfoot culture was then still very active on the reserve, allowing young women to dress up quite colourfully, taking great pride in their personalized beadwork designs and costume adornment. What a contrast to the plain uniforms and outfits seen here and in other scenes. Collection of Glenbow Archives

" *One day I told the Principal of St. Paul's Residential School, the Rev. Canon Middleton, how disappointed I was that none of our native Indian Canadian boys or girls had been invited to London, England. As they were the real Canadians, they should be present at the coronation of their majesties...to represent Canada. A few days later the Rev.....received a telegram....saying 'send a girl student to London.'*

*"We were requested to send a student with academic
standing, also good health and appearance. We had
many students in the school who could answer to all
these requirements. But one student had to be chosen.
The Rev.... and I decided that Nora Gladstone was the
girl."*

Being also from England, Canon Middleton was no doubt as
proud as the nurse that one of their students was going. To an-
nounce this news, he made a dramatic presentation one day to all
the students and staff, after they had completed Evensong together in the chapel. He described to them the many sights and
sounds that one would experience in attending the upcoming
Coronation - which was a great event even for Indian households.

*The imposing red face of St. Paul Anglican School's main
building has intimidated many a young Blood child sent to live
here after family life in a small cabin. Students in uniform
flank visiting dignitaries, who are being hosted by Archdea-
con S.H. Middleton (at centre, in black cloth) and Nurse Jane
Megarry (at left, in white).*
Collection of Glenbow Archives

He talked quite awhile, as he was known for doing, making everyone in the crowd daydream about going there. Then, when he had them spellbound, he let them know that someone in their midst was actually going to be going. Finally, he named Nora Gladstone.

> *"Nora was very popular with the staff and pupils, but the boys were very much disappointed because one of them had not been chosen to go.*
> *"Nora was the second daughter of Mr. & Mrs. James Gladstone, a very popular and charming couple (he later became Canada's first Indian senator to the capital in Ottawa). Chief Joe Healy, Minor Chief of the Blood Indian tribe, and his charming wife - Nora's grandfather and grandmother - were very popular with both Indian and white people. Anyone who called at their home received a very hearty welcome at all times.*
> *"There was much excitement in the school, for in two weeks Nora would be leaving St. Paul's, travelling in the train to Eastern Canada, then crossing the mighty ocean in a ship to England. What experiences and thrills and how many strange and wonderful sights Nora would see, and how many interesting stories she would tell when she returned to her home and loved ones in her beloved Canada -*
> *"We gave a party at the school for Nora, a few nights before she left. Her father, mother, brothers and sisters and other relations and friends, and the staff and pupils of the school were present. Nora was presented with many useful gifts, everything she would require on her journey.*
> *"Nora thanked everyone for their kindness...she then left the auditorium - and returned a few minutes later in her lovely ceremonial dress of white buckskin, with leggings and moccasins, all embroidered with many beautiful coloured beads. She also wore a necklace and bracelets of white wampum. On her lovely shining black hair she wore a glittering beaded headband, with two feathers -*

*the eagle plume that crests the head of Indian Chieftains.
Nora looked like a fairy Indian princess that night. She
recited "Canadian Born," and "As Red Men Die," two
poems written by the late Pauline Johnson, Canada's be-
loved Indian poet princess. Nora recited the poems with
such feeling that it brought tears to the eyes of many that
were present at that happy gathering.*

*"As we were making the final preparations for Nora's de-
parture, her mother came to me one day and said she
thought Nora would not be going to London as arranged. I was surprised and disappointed at the sudden
news. I said, 'Mrs. Gladstone, you surely don't mean to
tell me Nora has got cold feet?' 'Oh no,' she said, 'nothing like that. She has heard that the chief is very angry
she is going to London. He thinks a boy should go, not a
girl, to represent the Blood Indian tribe at the coronation of their majesties.' Nora did not care to offend the
head Chief of the Blood tribe. She knew and respected
the tribal law. But it was explained to the head Chief that
we had been asked to send a girl, though he would have
still preferred a boy.*

*It took a while for
Blood chiefs to accept
that the first tribal delegate ever sent to a
royal coronation in
England would be this
pleasant girl - Nora
Gladstone - instead of a
man, or at least a boy.
Here she is on the
steps of St. Paul's
School, dressed as she
was to meet their ma-
jesties in 1937.*
Collection of Glenbow
Archives

*"The morning for Nora's departure arrived. Mr. John
Pugh, Indian Agent on the Blood Reserve, arrived at St.
Paul's school in his motor car to drive Nora, her father*

and mother, and me to Calgary.... She was given a won-
derful send-off by the staff and pupils.

"As the train steamed slowly away from the station (in
Calgary) amid ringing cheers, it was a lovely sight to see
the happy smiling faces of those eager young girls. The
chosen few of the rising generation of the youth of Cana-
da.

"The girls had a very happy time on board ship - the
captain and crew were all very kind to them. The girls
were given parties and concerts, for which Nora donned
her white buckskin dress and beaded headband with the
two eagle feathers.

"Nora said everything was so strange and new to her - so
small in comparison to the vast land of Canada. The
trains in England were so small and swift; in Canada the
trains were long, with large engines. She loved the Eng-
lish country homes, the green lawns, the lovely valleys
and country lanes, the beauties of old churches and ca-
thedrals.

"The Canadian Indian students were taken to and shown
everything of interest in London and many other places
in England and Scotland. They wandered down the
aisles of Westminster Abbey and St. Paul's Cathedral
and the English House of Parliament. They visited many
schools and were honored guests.

"Seats were arranged for the visiting students from many
lands, in front of Buckingham Palace; they all had a
wonderful view of the royal procession. They cheered
heartily for their majesties, the king and queen as they
passed slowly by. She also said, 'When the Royal Cana-
dian Mounted Police passed by in their brilliant scarlet,
gold and blue uniforms we Canadians gave them a spe-
cial cheer - we were very proud of them.'

"While in London, Nora spoke to the British people
through the BBC microphone. She was among the youth
of the empire in the Albert Hall where they were all greet-
ed by Prime Minister Stan Baldwin. The king and queen

*and other members of the royal family were presented at
that great gathering.*

*"Nora was presented to England's noble daughter - the
stately and very gracious Queen Mary - at Marlborough
House. She said Queen Mary was very kind and gracious
and lovely, but when she smiled she was beautiful!*

*"When Nora returned to Canada she was guest speaker
at many meetings, telling large crowds of people all
about her visit to England and her impressions of the
British people, all the historic and scenic places and of
the pageantry of the royal procession.*

*"When Nora returned to her home on the Blood Reserve
she was given a wonderful reception by the head chief,
Shot-on-Both-Sides and minor chiefs and members of the
tribe. They were all very proud of her and they honored
her by giving her the rank of Princess and they named
her Nin-Aki, which means First Woman. This was done
with full ceremony, carrying with it the same rank and
honour of the Blood Indian tribe that are bestowed on
the wife of the Governor-General of Canada or the wife
of the President of the United States. She takes precedence over all other women of the Blood tribe. Miss Nora
Gladstone - Princess Nin-Aki - is the first Blood Indian
woman upon whom the rank of Princess has been con-
ferred."*

Perhaps we should pause here to explain the facts, now that
Nurse Megarry is letting romantic enthusiasm get her carried
away. In the context of Nora Gladstone's age, she certainly was
highly honored in the tribe. Public name-giving ceremonies by
the Head Chief were indeed usually reserved for the likes of
Governor-Generals and Presidents. Their wives were usually honored by the tribe's leading women, but not by the head chief.
However, the title of "Princess" did not exist in Blackfoot culture, nor did the notion of royalty. As far as her leading rank
and precedence, she would still have been seen as a young girl
by the Sun dance holy women, by women who were keepers of

certain Medicine Bundles, and by the members of sacred socie-
ties, none of whom she was qualified to be ahead of in any way.
It would be more accurate to say that Nora Gladstone established
a special place of her own within the tribe, and for that accom-
plishment, the unique title of princess was no doubt quite appro-
priate. In fact, today many young Indian girls compete eagerly
for the privilege of being named Princess on behalf of school or
social organizations. At pow-wows one often sees a half dozen or
more such native "nobility," wearing beaded dresses and head-
bands like Nora, often leading the crowds of dancers for their
spectacular "grand entries."

The Indian princess who went to see the King and Queen is
now a retired widow named Nora Baldwin, living near her son
and grandchildren in British Columbia, not far from the Van-
couver General Hospital where she spent 23 years working as a
nurse - the first one of our people to work in this occupation.
According to her, it wasn't an easy goal to reach.

> *"In order to pursue my chosen careen in nursing I need-
> ed to get a regular high school diploma, so I applied to
> attend public school in Cardston. This town is built on
> land taken from our tribe by the Mormons, yet because I
> was an Indian they wouldn't let me attend their school.
> This was in 1937. So I went to school in Saskatoon in-
> stead, far from home and feeling very lonesome. But that
> still wasn't the end of it. I applied to a hospital in Van-
> couver where I wanted to do my nurses' training, but the
> person in charge said, "What will our patients say when
> they know they're being treated by an Indian?" Fortu-
> nately, the Royal Jubilee Hospital in Victoria, B.C. took
> me instead.*
>
> *"The trip to see the King and Queen has always been a
> highlight in my life - I think about it most every day.
> There were 150 of us from native tribes. There was a
> pow-wow held on the reserve after I got back, during
> which I was nonoured by our old head chief Shot-on-
> Both Sides, who was helped by World War I veteran Mike*

Mountain Horse in placing an eagle feather war bonnet on my head. Nurse Megarry wrote that she thought they then named me "Ninnaki," which means Chief Woman (the Blackfoot word for the Queen). They may have said something about me being a "chief woman" for going on such a long journey, but as I recall the name they actually gave me was more like "Travelling a long ways across the Big Water."

Nora (Gladstone) Baldwin, almost fifty years after her memorable trip to the royal coronation. Besides being the first delegate from the Blood tribe at such an event, she also went on to become our first working nurse. The photo was taken on the day of her retirement in 1985.
Nora Baldwin Collection

8.

Traditional Ways With Children
From Margaret Hind Man (Ah'-dunn)

There are just a few elders of Margaret Hind Man's generation left among the Blood people these days and hardly any who
were raised as traditionally as she was. My mother was fortunate
to have spent a lot of time around her own buffalo-era grandmother, but even she doesn't hesitate to say that her good friend
Ah'-dunn grew up "a lot more Indian."

What did it mean a few decades ago to "live Indian" on a reservation? For Ah'-dunn it meant speaking our native Blackfoot
language at home to her husband and children, being generous
and kind, especially to her elders, wearing dresses, long hair in
braids, cooking simple meals that centered around meat, with
bread and potatoes in place of our earlier reliance on wild plants
and roots. For Ah'-dunn, it also meant knowing those plants and
roots, how to find them and what to do with them, as part of
keeping alive our tribal relationship with things of the land.

It wasn't until her older age that Ah'-dunn began to take an
active part in ceremonial dances and ceremonies. While younger,
she had faith and respect for these traditional religious ways, but
considered them the sacred domain of her elders. In those times
people did not simply join in when ceremonies were taking
place, but went only if specifically invited by the leaders and
sponsors. She has now been twice the holder of the sacred tri-
pods for medicine bundles, and also a member of the Motokiks,
a sacred women's society handed down from the buffalo days.

Not many people today have traditional knowledge of how
our people were born in the past, or such details as the traditional
raising of children, how they were taught and disciplined. Here is
what Ah'-dunn says on these subjects.

"I learned about childbirth by helping when my older sister had her baby at home. The widow of an old man named White Calf was living near us, and she knew about childbirth as an Indian midwife. She took care of my sister with herbal brews. She would use her own special plants, preparing them while singing her power song and praying, after which she made her drink the mixture down.

"When the time finally arrived for the baby to come out, that old lady again sang her song, then suddenly the baby just came out. Right after that, she told my sister to kneel, then she held her tight around the middle of the waist and she kept rubbing downward until the afterbirth was out. She tied the umbilical cord, after first squeezing one part of it in two opposite directions from the point where she was going to tie it off and then cut it.

"The newborn baby wasn't washed right at first; that old lady just wiped it clean and then rubbed it; I don't know if she used face cream or real fat, but she rubbed the baby on its feet and hands, then all over its body. After that she wrapped the umbilical cord in a little circle so that it looked kind of like a sausage. Then she tied a long strip of soft cloth around the baby's middle in such a way that it also covered and held down that wrapped-up cord, after which she bundled the baby up in a soft blanket. she didn't put any clothes on it at this time.

"My sister was put on a bed afterwards, with a pillow at each end, but that old lady wouldn't let her lay still for too long, nor go to sleep. There were a couple of old women there with her all night, brewing a big pot of coffee and making her drink some to stay awake. There was still blood inside her; they kept her moving around so that it wouldn't coagulate. They'd make her get up and put her head to the other end of the bed and then back again, just to keep her moving. It was until after this that I saw her nursing her baby.

"I learned that in the old days when a mother couldn't

*nurse, she fed her baby from her own mouth by letting
fluids drip slowly into the baby's mouth. The baby would
be sucking on the lip while pulling the liquid into its
mouth. I once fed a motherless puppy that way myself,
after my daughter brought it home and cried when I
wanted to get rid of it. That night I put some sugar in a
cup of tea and kept it by where I slept. Whenever the
puppy woke up and cried during the night, I would take
a drink and pass it on to the pup. He would drink as it
dripped from my lips and then go back to sleep. Later we
got a baby bottle to feed it.*

*"When I was small I played with puppies as if they were
my babies. I would even wrap them up in a little imita-
tion blanket as if they were children. Although we didn't
keep dogs inside our home normally, my parents would
not chase me out with one of these 'puppy babies.' They
would treasure it, instead. One of them would say, 'Oh,
that's her dog, put something out for it,' then they'd give
it a special treat and let it eat in the house. Dogs were
the special friends of women back in the old times. We
learned from them, by watching their actions, they were
like scouts and guards. Besides that, they carried our belongings, especially in the times before we had horses.*

*"In those days children acted very different from now;
they were much more behaved and disciplined. They
didn't cry and fuss all the time like so many children do
now. It was a hard and dangerous life. If there was any
disturbance, a child would just be nudged and right
away it would be quiet. I have a grandson that I raised
in this sort of way; sometimes I just wave at him and he'll
know to be quiet.*

*"When they were attacked in the old days, a woman
would just point her child in a certain direction and they
would flee, with no words spoken. If there were more
than one, the woman would put the youngest child on
her back and the rest will help each other. They'll run
along quickly, with no crying or screaming."*

Ah'-dunn says this sort of very disciplined behaviour among children had already changed by her time in the 1920's, forty years after the wild life of our tribe ended and we got peacefully settled. Yet even to this day when you drive up as a stranger to one of the more traditional family houses on the reserve you're likely to see small children scurry quickly out of sight, waiting somewhere nearby to see how the adults inside their home react, before they themselves come closer or get relaxed. On the other hand, Ah'-dunn feels that far too many kids nowadays are too sassy and don't seem to hear well; she says it compares poorly with our tribal past, in which children never talked back or acted smart with grownups. Here are some more of her thoughts from that time.

> *"The way that we got our names back in my time was from the old men who went on the war trails. For instance, in my family I had a grandfather named Iron Necklace who had been a good warrior, so he named many of us children, to pass on his good luck. He named me Little Gun Woman, for the first kind of gun he ever captured from an enemy.*
>
> *"A yellow bird spoke to my grandfather in his dreams and gave him power, so he named another one of us Yellow Bird. Although he named me Little Gun, I've always been call Ah'-dunn, although that's really just a nickname. My mother was always saying about me 'Ni'-dunn,' which* in Blackfoot means 'my daughter,' *but my brother could only pronounce it as 'Ah'-dunn,' so that's how it stuck, and I'm still using it today. I like my name, so I'm stingy with it.*
>
> *"My brother's Indian name was Butterfly. The way we gave him this was by changing his formal name of Bernard to 'Ah'-bunneh,' which sounds similar and is Blackfoot for Butterfly.*
>
> *"It was before my time when the women and girls always wore buckskin dresses, although I often heard about it. Back then they always saved the thickest and softest piec-*

*es of tanned hide and they cut these sort of like a small
apron, and that is what they used during their monthly
periods. When it was soiled, a girl or woman would go
off by herself and she would lay it out and let it dry, then
after that she would scrape it clean with a rough rock, so
she could put it back on again. It's new to us how they
make these pads that they put there now. In the Blackfoot
language we still say, 'I'm going out to scrape myself,'
but of course we don't use pieces of hide anymore.*

*"During their period, it was expected for women to spend
their time quietly and not go around. They were not allowed into ceremonies or near certain sacred things.
Some girls were spoken of as being too lively, and it was
said that you could see their trail, which was considered
disgraceful. In my young days we were still taught man-
ners like that, but now very few people know about them,
or care.*

*"When a girl was ready to be married, her family and
relatives gathered goods and property, then they drove
the girl with them to the chosen husband. Generally she
wasn't asked, but some of them wouldn't agree to it when
they found out who it was; they'd wrap up in their shawls
and sleep by the door instead of with their new husbands. Others would jump up and run back to their parents and homes. I guess some of these were too young
and not yet ready to have mates.*

*"We learned from our mothers and grandmothers how to
prepare food and how to use all the parts of an animal
that a hunter brings home, from the head to the legs and
tail. For instance, when all the meat is gone from the leg
of an animal like the buffalo or an elk, you can break the
bone, then take a willow stick and peel the bark from one
end to make a kind of a brush, and with that you dig into
the bone for the marrow; you suck it from that stick. In
the old days this was something like their candy.*

*"Before breaking the leg bone for marrow, we would
take off the skin, along with the small hooves, and these*

*pieces we sewed together to make saddle bags for when
they moved their camping gear around. The women
would ride on her horse and put one of these leg bags
behind her, full of her important things. Other ones of
these were sewn together in a pail-form, to make contain-
ers for gathering berries or to store their tools.*

*By the early part of the
1900's our people only used
buckskin clothing for special occasions, but girls
still wore "traditional
dresses" most of the time.
This is Sleeping in the Water, a real "daughter of buffalo women," whose mother
used to tan the hides
brought home by her father,
Flying About. The girl later
married a noted Blood named
Big Nose.*
Collection of Good Medicine
Foundation

"*In a similar way we used the heads of animals to make
bags. They were skinned, then all the openings were sewn
shut, after which they were stuffed with wild grass and left
hanging outside to dry. A string was added at the open
end, then a girl would use it for picking berries. Big animal heads were used in this fashion by the women, while
the smaller heads were used by girls. They would also use
them to store their pemmican, a snack food made from
berries, crushed meat, and fat.*
"*They scraped the hair from the animal hides that they
tanned, and they sewed that hair into long, thin bags*

*that they used like mattresses, and they made pillows in a
similar way. Also, along the legs there is sinew that's
thick and straight, which they dried and used like an awl
for sewing, along with the sinew from the backbone. That
was before we got such things as needles, but for some
kinds of work they still used sinew in my time. It was very
strong thread for sewing.*

*"They didn't have many children in the old days, often
just one or two. Life was very hard for mothers who were
carrying children, so they lost them easily. Some had the
power to "tie" women so that they'd never have children
again. I've always suspected my old mother-in-law had
that power and used it on me. When I was young I just
had my one daughter, and after that this old lady said,
"I don't want her to have any more children.' And sure
enough, after that there was always something wrong
with me when I wanted to have more kids, so in the end, I
never did.*

*"Although I experienced these kinds of things, by the
time my mother raised me life was starting to get a little
more modern for us. For instance, both my parents had
already been to school, although not for very long. The
area where I grew up was at the north end of our reserve,
where the Many Tumors clan of our family lived. Among
our neighbors were the families of Berry Child and Gets
Another Gun.*

*"One of my earliest memories is of the spring-time, when
we left our home and moved east further out onto the
prairie, where the men worked in the fields cutting hay
and so forth. We would live in a canvas tent put up next
to a wooden granary there. This was to help protect our
camp from the wind. When it got too windy, our family
would go inside the granary for shelter, although my
mother cooked only in the tent. Sometimes I got fright-
ened by the strong winds, out in the open.*

*"In those times my clothing was what you could call tra-
ditional Blackfoot style. I wore a "real dress" which is*

*our name for the clothing made from the original kind of
wool cloth brought to us by early traders. With this I
wore a leather belt, a coat or jacket when it was cold,
and always a fringed shawl over my shoulder, pinned at
the neck. You could see us young girls chasing each other and playing out on the prairie, our shawls flapping so
that we must have looked funny. I also remember very
well that we wore knitted hats of a kind that you don't
see around anymore.*

*"There were two places in those times where we did most
of our shopping. Up at the north end where we lived it
was the store run by R.N. Wilson, whom we named Long-
Nosed Crow, while down east they had another store run
by a man known as Cree Talker, because he spoke that
language. Besides buying our basic food and supplies,
we also went to the store to pick up our mail.*

*"It was from the store run by Long-Nosed Crow that I got
my first pair of shoes, leather ones with high tops and
buttons on the sides. Before that I wore only moccasins,
which my mother usually made for me. I also got my
shawls from that store and I recall that as a small girl I
always looked through them to see what new colors and
patterns they had on hand.*

*"When I got to be about six, most of the other children I
knew got sent to school, but my parents kept me at home.
I think of the Anglican Canon Middleton as a bad man,
because when I was young he would come around and
just forceably take children away from their parents.*

*"Sometimes he brought along some of the police, and he
would threaten to arrest parents if they didn't go along
with his demands. He came for my brother First Gun and
me, but my father just told him, "They will go to school
when their time comes; I have already thought about it.'
Canon Middleton agreed to wait, although at first my father sent only my brother. He was there for a couple of
years before I was sent to follow him.*

"My first stay in school was not for long, as I got sick

*and my parents took me back home. My father said, 'You
will not go to school anymore; it has not been good for
you.' But the problem was that my best friend was at
school, so I had no one to play with and I wanted to be
there too. This girl was Cougar Head's daughter and her
name was Nosey. Finally I got so lonesome for her that I
snuck away and went back to school, which was my second time. I stayed for two years, and that is when I
learned to speak English. Although I wasn't there long,
had I not snuck away I might never have learned to
speak it, and sure not to read and write, since my parents
at home spoke only Blackfoot and there was nothing
around to read.*

"*After my second time at school I went back home and
spent most of my time with my mother, whom we called
Doh-watskie, though I'm not sure how to translate it.
Those are her ways that I follow in my own life. Although
I learned a lot from her, she never said to me, 'Do this
and do that.' that's not our traditional way of learning.
Instead, I just watched the way she did things; I learned
by watching, and by helping, She really knew the ways of
our buffalo times.*

"*For instance, in the summer when berries were ripe my
mother would start out by gathering saskatoons, because
they become ripe first. We picked quite a lot of them; she
would clean them, then spread them out on a sheet of
canvas to dry. When they got a bit hard, only partly
dried, she would rub some fat on her hands and then all
over the berries, after which she spread them back out to
dry the rest of the way. That was her method of drying
these favorite berries. That's an example of the kinds of
things I learned from my mother, that I wouldn't have
learned at school.*

"*Chokecherries ripen later in the summer. At that time my
mother would go to her in-law whose name was Barely-
Being-Heard, because berries grew real good there. We
would pick them for a while, then she would start crush-*

*ing the wild cherries with her stone hammer. When they
were well crushed, seeds and all, she would put them into
a bowl. That's how we brought them home in the evening; she would just leave them outside in that bowl
overnight, up where animals couldn't get to it. The next
day she did the same again, spreading out a sheet of
canvas, then she'd start shaping the crushed chokecherries into patties that she layed out to dry. She turned
these regularly until they were really dry, then she put
them into white flour sacks. Sometimes she was able to fill
two big sacks with these wild cherry patties.*

*"She also dried some of the chokecherries whole, with
the pits still in them. When they started to get wrinkled
she put them into sacks to finish drying. And the other
way, she also crushed some saskatoons and made them
into patties, like the ones with chokecherries. Usually she
mixed a bit of flour in with them; she used the dried flour
and berry patties for making a real good berry soup.
These different methods that she used added variety to
her simple foods.*

*"Nowadays when I'm planning to go berry picking, I
buy netting in town and I use it to dry my berries. First I
wash them, then I spread them out on canvas, and finally
I cover them with the netting. That way the flies won't
land on them. I really hate flies because I find them so
bothersome; and here we cannot even eat them!*

*"My mother also gathered different wild roots to dry for
later cooking and eating. Our favorite was maas, the
Blackfoot name for wild turnip, which grows mainly on
sidehills. You could see them afterwards, hanging all
over at people's homes while they were drying. My mother bagged these too; with her prepared wild foods she
could reach the next summer. From her I learned a lot
about our different old ways.*

*"Eventually came the time for me to leave my mother and
get married. In keeping with our customs, we went to live
with my husband's family. We couldn't live with my fami-*

ly because my husband and mother were not allowed to speak with each other, or even to be in the same room. It took me a while to get used to this, but I had a good husband and his family was nice to me.

Here is Margaret Hind Man (known in our language as Ah'-dunn), standing with her husband Walter in front of their tipi in 1977. This lodge was decorated with the buffalo-hoof design which was ceremonially transferred to them.
Adolf Hungry Wolf Photo

"My husband's old folks prayed all the time, it seemed. I remember the old lady getting up in the morning, first thing, to go outside and pray; I would lay in bed listening to her words. She was glad to see a new day, and she gave thanks for it. If someone got up mad, she would tell them, 'What's this - you are not glad to see a new day?'
"In the night time I would hear her pray as well; she would ask for a peaceful night for all of us, for nothing bad to happen to us during the darkness, and for us to

*have a nice morning. I never heard her using harsh
words to talk to anyone; she never swore; she always
spoke gently and tried to live by her prayers.*

*"Those are happy memories for me; it makes me lone-
some to recall those times. Now that I have some wisdom
in my old age, I find my children to be a great loss because they have died. I always thought I would be very
good to my children, that I would make a good path for
them, but it didn't happen that way. My husband and I
didn't take up drinking liquor, we didn't swear, and we
tried not to talk mean. I just followed him and together
we had an easy and gentle life. Maybe because of that,
my grandchildren seem to be shy of me; they have respect for me. Sometimes all my grandchildren come to
visit me, especially on the weekends, and then I'm happy
to have a full house. This is the main reward of my long
life and I'm very thankful for it."*

9.

My Aunt Next Door
From Mabel Beebe (Sacred Buffalo Stone Woman)

My mom and her brother have raised their families within sight of each other on land where their mom and dad raised them. Uncle Howard and Aunt Mabel were our nearest relatives and neighbors.

When I was little I remember my aunt's old mother praying for all of us while she was holding a little piece of meat aloft as an offering. This left a deep impression on me and was one of my first tastes of our traditional religion. One of us was told to bring that piece of meat outside and put it into the ground. Years later, when my own kids were small, we found our place on the tribal tipi camp circle to be right next to this old woman for the annual Sun Dance gathering, so that I was able to have some very rewarding visits with her. As the former keeper, with her husband White Man Left, of both a Beaver Medicine Bundle and a Medicine Pipe Bundle, I especially valued her comments on guidance during my own first years with both duties.

Although my Aunt Mabel grew up around her mother's ceremonial life, she was involved in more modern endeavors for most of her adulthood. My uncle Howard was a lifetime Chief in the old system, under Head Chief Shot-on-Both-Sides, back when I was small. Later he served several elected terms when our tribe took on newer political ways. He was also an important organizer and elected officer in the Indian Association of Alberta, one of the first inter-tribal political groups formed in our country. All this work kept my uncle very busy, and frequently travelling, with my aunt giving him full support and often travelling with him. In fact, because of this she became one of the first women in our tribe to visit so many far away and foreign places.

My aunt's first airplane trip with my uncle resulted in a funny anecdote that got told in our family for years. It seems she had the window seat, so my uncle leaned over her to look and point things out. Just then the plane banked sharply to that side, which scared my aunt and made her tell my uncle, "sit back up and quit tilting the plane."

> *"My mother and father split up when I was only four days old and I was left with my mother. We stayed with my grandfather until my mother got remarried to a man named Mistaken Chief, who raised me so that I thought for many years he was my real father.*
> *"For some reason my own father never bothered with me until I was about five, when he started sending the Catholic priest to get me enrolled at St. Mary's School. My stepfather told the priest to wait a while, that I was too young, so he left. But he came back another time, again and again. One time it was Father Ruaux, and he had along a couple of nuns and a couple of women from our tribe. I remember that they brought a bunch of food for my parents, bread and other stuff, because they wanted to persuade my parents to turn me over to them. I didn't get to hear the conversation they had about it, because as soon as my stepfather saw them coming in the distance, he took me out of the house the other way and we went over to visit his brother Striped Wolf, who lived nearby. The priest only got to see my mother and my grandfather.*
> *"When these people said why they came, my grandfather told Father Ruaux, 'These people are the ones that raised the girl; the real father never paid anything or helped out. Mistaken Chief and her mother are the ones to decide when and where she goes to school.' The priest didn't like that; he kept trying to say my real father wanted me in the Catholic school right away. Finally my mother answered firmly that she wasn't letting me go until I got a little older, so he gave up and left. In those days a lot of kids never went to school until they were nine or ten, and some were even older.*

*"That following spring we had a real unpleasant en-
counter with my dad on one of the reserve roads. We had
just received our five dollars each that the government
gave out for treaty money, and we were on our way down
to Mr. Wilson's store to do some shopping. I was riding
in the back of our horse-drawn democrat when we met
up with him; as soon as I heard who it was I crawled under the seat to hide, I was so scared of him. We stopped
to say hello, and soon they were all arguing about me. I
had just turned seven, and he was saying I should be in
school, while my mom thought I should wait a little longer yet. He got mad and started swearing, calling my father down, making me even more scared of him.*

*"After that encounter my mother went to see her relative
Percy Creighton, who was one of the tribe's minor chiefs.
He told her, 'Just put her in St. Paul's School, the one
run by the Anglicans, rather than the Catholic school my
real dad wanted. He said, 'Otherwise that man will keep
bothering you, and if you put her in the school that he
wants then in the end he will steal her away from you.'
When my mother agreed, he and Jim Gladstone came to
our house and brought me to St. Paul's school.*

*"So that's when my school life began, and I was scared
of it at first. Sure enough, we were mistreated right from
the start, but not by the school staff. It was the older girls
from our own reserve who mistreated us, ones who had
already finished their schooling and were working as
matrons, acting like supervisors. They had favorites
whom they treated real well, their own relations, or the
girlfriends of their younger brothers. I was not one of
these, so I suffered from them. For instance, my mom and
dad would buy me ribbons and barrets to wear - nice
barrets, with stones on them - but these older matron
girls would just take them away from me, leaving me to
cry.*

*"In 1924 the town of Fort Macleod had its Jubilee,
which was a really big event for everybody in this region,*

*Indian and white. They had a big fair ground, and all us
kids from the school were brought there to take part in
the fun. But then I ran into my real dad, and he wanted
me to go around with his family, though I refused. I
stayed right next to our matron after that, being scared
that my dad might steal me away. The next day when the
kids were taken from the school to Fort Macleod again, I
decided not to go, along with another girl, so the two of
us stayed behind with the school cook. I remember that
time well because she fed us really good, and there was
no one around to bother us.*

*"For Christmas of that same year they sent all us young-
er children home, while the older ones helped the school
staff to move into our new buildings. That was a big
change and it sure made my time at school a lot more
enjoyable. For one thing, we no longer had to use outside toilets; on real cold nights it used to be miserable for
us to have to go out back. We'd come back in nearly fro-
zen, standing around the big stove trying to warm up.
Those who were favored got to stand right next to the
stove - they could almost sit on top of it - while the rest of
us never get a chance to get that near so it took us a lot
longer to get warm.*

*"One time I was on the school veranda looking out
through the windows when one of those older girls came
up and scratched me. It was really bleeding, so when I
got asked about it I said, 'That big girl sure is mean.'
For saying that, the same girl took a branch and started
hitting me in the face with it, giving me a real beating.*

*"The favorites of those older girls caught on to this mean
treatment and gave us some of it themselves. They'd
stand around at the top of a flight of stairs and wait for
us other little kids to come by, then they'd push us down
so that we'd tumble and fall. I used to have bruises from
it all the time, and it's a wonder that none of us ever
broke our legs or arms.*

"Because of all this mistreatment by the older girls from

*our own tribe, I really didn't like school too well when I
was small, though I knew that my parents wanted me to
go there. They'd have a hard time getting me to go back,
each time I went home for a break or vacation. I didn't
tell my parents what was going on with those girls, so
they knew nothing about it.*

*"At the new school they no longer allowed us to speak
Indian at all. One of those big girls carried around a
chalk board on which she'd write down every Indian
word that any of us said, then she would report us to the
school staff and we'd get punished for it. So it was our
own kind who helped force us away from our native language.*

*"But eventually as I got older and better able to protect
myself, school became more enjoyable. They started
teaching us how to work, making us help out in the laundry, kitchen, bakery, sewing room; we'd work in shifts
and change each week to something different, so I really
liked that; then I didn't hate school anymore.*

*"After I turned twelve they didn't let us go home any-
more at all, even for vacations. At that stage they wanted
to keep us away from the boys, so every summer during*

**Blood girls from St. Paul's School are seen with their super-
visor arriving at the summer camp by Waterton Lakes National
Park, about 1922. In this case the journey included a ride
aboard one of the area's first trucks.**
Collection of Glenbow Archives

Nurse Megarry's students looked forward to the breaks she gave them from their daily boarding school routines. Here they are having a picnic on the open prairies, where their grandmothers camped and tanned buffalo robes just a few years earlier.
Collection of Glenbow Archives

school break they brought all us older girls to the mountains, to land that the tribe owns just outside of Waterton Lakes National Park. We all had a good time there together, and we sort of lost touch with what was going on anywhere else. We lived in a cottage up there and spent a lot of our time swimming, hiking and doing other outdoor things. Sometimes were were given boat rides up and down the lakes, which was a new experience for us. We also went berry picking and even mountain climbing. We got to see and know about wild animals, including bears, of which there were quite a few nearby. Sometimes deer would come right up to us and eat from our hands. I was always sad when our summer days of mountain camping were over.

"During this time I grew quite close to Nurse Megarry, who was really kind and taught me many valuable things. She was like a second mother to us, and she treated us as kindly as if we were her own children. She did special things with us on all the main holidays, and this made our time at school much more enjoyable.

"Unfortunately, at about this time I started having eye problems, and in the end that brought a close to my schooling, though I've always been sorry about it. The problem started while we were spring cleaning at the school, helping to wash the staff room. We were pulling

down the drapes when something got in my eye that really hurt. I was brought to the nurse and she tried washing it out, but the pain wouldn't go away. Had Canon Middleton taken me to town right away for treatment by a doctor, I think my eye would have been alright. But he was boss, and after he looked at it they just kept me in a dark room, figuring it would get better.

"This was in June, when we were supposed to write our exams, but my eye hurt too much so I wasn't able to take part. Then they brought us girls back up to the mountains by Waterton Lakes, but this time I couldn't enjoy any of it. While the girls went out and had fun, I had to stay at the cottage where it wasn't too bight for my eye. You'd think that by this time they'd have brought me to a doctor, but that wasn't the case.

"By August my eye did finally improve enough so that I could think about going to classes. Canon Middleton decided I should continue with the rest of my classmates into grade eight, though I still hadn't done the exams for grade seven. They said if I finished grade eight they would send me to a school in Northern British Columbia where I could get nurse's training, which is what I really wanted.

"Around October my eye started getting bad again, so they finally brought me to the hospital in Lethbridge and I don't remember how long I stayed there before they cured the problem. Then a relative of mine named First Rider came and said to me, 'You will come home with us; you will not stay in school until you are an old lady.' He had never been to school himself, so he had a very old fashioned view about it. When I got to their house, he and my grandmother started reviewing all the eligible bachelors, saying 'He comes from this and this family,' reviewing his family history to see if he'd make a good husband for me. I really hated when they started talking like that, and they were very serious.

"When we went to Mass that New Year's, I asked Canon

*Middleton if I could come back to the school, so he told
me, 'Of course, this is your home.' So at that point my
education continued. Also my social life, since they had
dances at the school every Friday night and I went to
them. Back with those old folks I could only go to Indian
dances, pow-wows but I found the other ones more fun.*
"*Around the end of January they always had a reunion
at St. Paul's School, and this time among the crowd was
an old lady named Mrs. Wings, who came over and told
me, 'So you're going to be our daughter-in-law.' I asked
her who, so she said, 'Howard Beebe; they have come
and asked him to be their son-in-law and he agreed.' I
wasn't even consulted, and I sure was unhappy about
that. I thought to myself, I'm really enjoying my stay here
at school, so why do I have to get married? But it was my
grandparent's wish and I couldn't refuse them.*
"*My grandparents prepared me in the old way and
brought me here to your uncle, where I've lived ever
since. Everything that I needed for a traditional marriage was provided by them, blankets, clothing, trunks
and a lot of other things. We got married legally way later, but at first it was done only the Indian way.*"

*My aunt Mabel Beebe is seen with my uncle Howard sitting in
the audience of the Blood tribe's annual Indian Days pow-wow
in 1982.*
Adolf Hungry Wolf Photo

10.

Leaving the Kitchen for Work
With Katie Wells (Little Woman Face)

Although Katie Wells and her family were not actually related to us, we all treated each other as if we were. I knew her throughout my young days since she lived just over the hill from our home and we were frequent visitors back and forth. For some reason, the one thing I remember best about her home was some kind of barometer that had been built into a miniature Bavarian house, from which a little carved couple sometimes came out. Something like this was unusual to see on the Blood Reserve at that time.

In our part of the reserve, Katie was the only mother and housewife who also had an outside job. For many years she worked at the St. Paul's Anglican School, staying there during the time that she worked and then coming home on her days off. She and her husband Dick Wells were a pretty progressive couple, so they owned a car when not too many people had one. Dick drove Katie to work in their car and picked her back up. I used to think she was quite rich, though now that I'm older I see that it was only in relation to others who lived right around her.

In some ways Katie and her husband were progressive like my aunt and uncle next door, but instead of travelling and dealing with politics, they worked at home and developed their farm. She was always a good housekeeper and seemed willing to try new things or ideas before most other women of her generation, which helped me to think of her as being rich. By this I don't necessarily mean with money, just that she had things that others sometimes didn't.

Like most Indian parents, Katie and her husband loved their children, and their children's friends. When I would go to play with her daughters, I was always impressed by the nice dolls and things that she had made for them. Every Christmas she and her husband would bag up a lot of candies that they then brought around to the various kids in our area, using their horses and a sleigh. The memories of seeing them in the snow like that are very special to me, something like the idea of Mr. and Mrs. Santa Claus.

"In the past, how we got food was very hard compared to nowadays. These new people don't know how difficult it was, everything goes so easy for them. These young girls just come in and cook something up in no time and they don't think much about it. In our time it was hard, so we valued all our food very highly, we looked after it.

"My mother and I used to go by team and wagon to get berries for the winter, and also roots. Then we used to get meat rations at the agency once a week, plus flour and some other things. It was good if you combined these rations with what you provided for yourself at home; if you knew how to manage it, you wouldn't be hard up. But if you just depended on the Indian agent you couldn't get very much.

"My dad had a little bit of education, so he knew how to work for himself. He had livestock, cows and horses, plus our farm and garden. We usually grew our own potatoes and stuff like that, then put them in our root house for winter. We kept most of our food in this root house, because back then we didn't keep the fire going in the stove all night, so things would freeze in our house. In years when we didn't have a garden, we'd buy the stuff for our root house from the Hutterites, or some other farmer.

"Berries the main food we always got and prepared ourselves; all different kinds of berries. Of course, the most important was saskatoon, and we dried these the same as everybody else, then boiled them through winter and mixed them in with other things. We made chokecherry patties and dried them in the sun, like they did in the past, but we also made some into preserves and even pancake syrup, which we learned to do at school and

*from other people. Sometimes we made saskatoon jam
and mixed it with rhubarb. Getting enough sugar to
sweeten our jams and canning was the hardest part, especially during the time of World War Two, when it was
really rationed.*

*"The popular drink back then was Coke; they were five
cents for a bottle, but only once in a blue moon did I get
to have a taste of it. My mother never had any fancy stuff
in our household in the way of food or sweets. The way
she used to be with me, I did the same for my children. If
they had candy, I put it way up on a shelf so they don't
eat it all up at once, and they don't keep crying for it.
Mostly I gave them fruit when they wanted a treat, so
they had good teeth for a long time. Nowadays we sure
ruin children's teeth by the candy and other sweet things
we feed them. As soon as a baby gets its first teeth, the
mother will just lay if down with a bottle in its mouth. The
baby falls asleep with this and the next thing you know
this tiny little kid has rotten teeth already.*

*"There was no such a thing as welfare back in my days. I
never knew of a person to go ask the government for welfare money, but today it is very easy to do this. The
young people have no experience with hardship the way
we had it in the past. It sure makes you appreciate life
much more.*

*"Even with the hardships, I found our life enjoyable. We
were never so hard up that we had to live in a tent or
tipi; we only used a tipi in the summer for the Sun Dance
camp. As far back as I can remember, my home was a
real good house. We had two bedrooms, a living room
and a kitchen, plus a storage room where my mom used
to put all her extra food and other stuff. I had a little sister, so there were two of us, plus our two older brothers.*

*"About the biggest fear that us kids had were the sick-
nesses that came around. Measles and chickenpox were
the two most common ones, and they seemed to hit us
about every second year. Sometimes we got whooping*

cough, which was pretty bad, and of course there was
always T.B., although not all that much of it. Still, when
the doctor came around in his team and wagon, all us
kids would go hide in the woods, because we were
scared.

"One of the worst things that came around was this in-
fluenza during the First World War, which killed a lot of
people on this reserve. It seemed like every day they went
to bury somebody. If people ate heavy food they would
die from it, though if they ate light food they usually got
better. Gradually everybody learned this and then the
epidemic went down. But for a time we had to wear
something to cover our mouths; when people came to
visit we had to wear sort of a net so we wouldn't exchange germs. It was really horrible for a while, something like that Aids.

"Whenever there was an outbreak of T.B. going around,
we'd be given cod-liver oil. They said it did something to
our lungs so that we wouldn't get sick. The kids were giv-
en this, sort of like a tonic. But if a child is fed right, I
find that it won't get sick often. If they are not fed properly, that has a lot to do with them getting sick.

"A few of my grandparents were still alive when I was
small, but not all of them. These were people from the
buffalo days, who still lived pretty much in their old fashioned ways. In fact, my sister was partly raised by our
grandmother Pipe Woman, who was from those old
times. She and another old lady named Cree Woman
were both married at the same time to my grandfather
Bull Shield, but I didn't know him. By the time my sister
stayed with her, Pipe Woman had been widowed and was
then married to another old timer named White Antelope.
I knew him very well and remember him as a very kind
and gentle man. One reason my sister stayed with them is
that our mother died young, when I was about nine years
old.

"There were several families in my time where the hus-

*bands had two wives. Eagle Child and Crow-Spreads-
His-Wings were among them. Nobody thought anything
of it; that's how our customs always were. But the missionaries wanted to put a stop to it, even though we
heard that the Mormons living right next to our reserve
had two or more wives themselves.*

*"In my own household I've had five children, all born at
the hospital. I had to go there several days early each
time, because all my deliveries were hard. The doctor
told me it was on account of my husband Dick, who was
kind of a big man, whereas I'm small. When I had the
fifth child, that was the end of it for me. I was about 32,
and having children just quit on its own. I was never sick
with it or anything; my periods were regular, but no
more kids. Then when I turned forty I noticed that I was
starting to have hot flashes. My aunt told me I was having a change of life. In March my periods ended until
October, and then they ended altogether, but I never he-
morrhaged. All I had was a little problem with my bones,
just for a short time. The pain was mostly in my back and
hips, but I went to the doctors in Lethbridge and they
worked on me until it got better.*

*"Not until I turned about 60 did it get worse again, this
time mainly in my feet, which really bothered me. Again
the doctors worked on me and made it feel better. Then it
went back to my knees and got so bad that I was just
about ready to start using a cane. But I kept trying
things, looking for remedies. It helped a lot to soak my
feet in hot water. Eventually I got better and left the cane
alone. But nowadays I get pretty sick sometimes when a
storm is brewing, though otherwise I'm still pretty fit.
What scares me most is the climbing up and down of
stairs. I really hold on tightly to the rails, because I'm
scared to slip and stumble. Stairs are very dangerous.
Old people shouldn't be on them at all.*

*"My husband and I worked hard together, right from the
start, to improve our life. Before we had our own farm,*

he used to work for ranchers in the area, all through the different seasons. He helped with plowing and planting, then he cut hay, then he went to help with the harvest, and when that was finished he went to the beet fields and worked there. Some of it I worked with him, like the sugar beets. It was a hard job, for which we got paid so much an acre. We'd save it up to get supplies for the winter.

Katie's husband Dick Wells is the handsome fellow sitting on the left in this 1927 portrait. Sitting next to him is George Good Dagger, while standing behind in the cowboy hat is "Long Jim" Takes-the-Gun-Strong and his buddy Albert Wolf Child. Their generation grew up hearing tales of buffalo hunting and warpath bravery in the lodges of old grandparents, yet circumstances forced them to support their own families through farming, ranching and other non-traditional work.
Collection of Good Medicine Foundation

"At first we lived in an old house up at the north end of the reserve, then we came down here and camped on this land where I raised my kids. We kept up our fences and seeded the fields. Eventually the chief and council offered us a new house, for which we had to pay $250 a year for ten years. We were very happy to get that, and to finally move out of that old place at the north end. Even though we only had wood and coal stoves, and no running water, we finally had a place to stay and settle down.

*"For quite a few years Dick plowed our own fields and
we were doing well. Then one day the Indian Department's farm instructor came and said to Dick, 'I think
you should let your horse go and start using the equipment that's coming down the road.' He explained how
the fancy new machinery could do a lot more work and
get bigger results. It meant the Indian Department would
come and do the work with these machines, instead of my
husband working our land. When the grain was sold that
came from our land, they took out the payments for this
machine first, then gave us the rest.*

*"Around the same time they brought a granary here, and
they told Dick that his job was to issue the spring wheat,
with me as his helper. We had to give so many bushels to
each person, depending on how much land they had. In
those days they didn't have very big farms, so we gave
out mostly around one or two hundred bushels. Dick had
a little scale that seemed so complicated, and with that
he weighed them. My job was to write down the names
and keep track of the amounts.*

*"But after a little while of this system, they came out and
told us the Blood tribe was broke, and that we'd have to
let some white ranchers come out and work our land in
order to pay off the debts. Just some of the reserve farmers caused this debt, and we weren't among them. Dick
didn't like the plan at all, and at first he wouldn't take
part in it. We were doing alright, and still paying off our
house, but after a couple of years they talked him into
turning the work over to others, as well.*

*"So they worked our land in order to help pay off the
debts caused by those other people, and for several years
we didn't get a cent. Dick was sure mad, because we had
to go out and find other jobs instead. There were no
more rations being given out, and welfare hadn't started
yet, so we had no choice but to work. I got myself a job
at the boarding school. For three years we worked like
that, then just before Christmas of the third year they told*

us that all the debts had been paid off and they gave us
$2,200 from our crops.

"That was a lot of money for us, all at once, so I told
Dick, 'Lets put it in the bank and it will be a good start
for saving more.' But he wouldn't listen to me, so he took
the money and bought a nice car with it instead. Boy, I
was mad at him for that, especially since he hardly knew
how to drive and didn't have a license. When he tried to
get one, he failed the test, though later he tried again
and passed it."

*Katie Wells, in her role as respected elder and grandmother,
riding on a float with an upcoming generation of Blood girls.
Tipis and buckskin dresses continue to be of important use in
Blackfoot culture, as seen here at the Blood Indian Days of
1980.*
Adolf Hungry Wolf photo

11.

A Medicine Pipe Ceremonial Elder
Molly Kicking Woman

*"We were quite young when we became bundle keepers,
my husband George and I; we were still in our twenties,
with small children. We didn't really know too much
about it. But the old folks of that time directed us; they
would say: 'This is what you will do.' And they would explain things to us: 'You will make incense for your medicine pipe bundle every morning and evening, and you
will pray with your pipe,' and so on. They didn't tell us
how to pray, they left that up to us. We listened to them,
since they prayed all the time, and that's how we learned
to pray, but they never told us what words to use."*

That's how Molly Kicking Woman recalls the start of a ceremonial career that has now spanned most of her lifetime, as she is
near eighty and the last old time leader of the women's part in
our important Medicine Pipe Bundle ceremonies. Note that I
didn't say she is the last leader, period; that's because there are
now several younger women also being called on as leaders. But
none of these received their initiations or training from a circle
of buffalo-era elders as Molly did. That makes her a landmark in
Blackfoot cultural history - when she goes, that part of our culture will be in completely new hands, mine among them.

Blackfoot Medicine Pipe Bundles have often been cared for
by the families of chiefs, so they became known as "chief's
bundles," though that wasn't an absolute requirement. Among
the many customs associated with these bundles is that, in the
past when camp was going to be moved, the people could tell in
which direction by looking to see where the pipe bundle and its
supporting tripod were standing in relation to the keeper's tipi,
early in the morning.

Molly's husband, George Kicking Woman, was for many years an elected member of the Blackfeet Tribal Council, so in our language he is called a chief. Thus he and Molly are among the last to practice the Blackfoot custom of "mixing religion with politics." George is noted for his honesty and integrity, qualities sadly lacking in so many modern-day politicians. Their annual Medicine Pipe Bundle ceremony, held for many years on Mother's Day, attracts hundreds of people from within the tribe and from distant places, many of them suffering ailments or other problems in life, thus coming to seek blessings and to gain strength. In their role of setting an example, Molly and George welcome everyone of any race; their door is always open. It is another traditional quality that is becoming harder to find.

As a child I recall going to visit relatives down on the Montana reservation, riding with my parents in their car, as they would point out the home of George and Molly Kicking Woman just outside the reservation town of Browning. One time I saw a big bunch of vehicles parked there, and I wondered what could be going on. I had no idea that they were having a Medicine Pipe ceremony, or even what it was, and certainly not that in a few more years I would be going there myself, bringing along my own children. Although we're not directly related, Molly sort of took me under her wing and taught me things as if I were her daughter, or a younger ceremonial sister.

"When I was young, back in the 1920's and 30's, we never travelled around much. The main place we used to go was up in Canada, to visit our North Peigan and Blood relatives. My mother and father had lots of family there, so we mostly went to be with them.

"Nowadays I hardly see any of the people that we used to visit, like Bad Eagle, Cat Woman, and the old Sun Dance woman, Mrs. Many Guns. Sometimes we would spend a whole month with them, camping in our own tent next to their homes.

"If there was a Sun Dance being put up while we were there, we'd move to it as well. Then, when the Sun Dance

*was over we'd go to the home of another of our relatives
and spend a few more weeks camped by them. Among the
Bloods it was often the home of my grandfather Many
Mules, or his adopted brother Steven Fox.*

*"In those days we did all our travelling by horse and
wagon. We had lots of time, and we travelled slowly. The
wagon had a sunshade that my mother sewed from canvas. She would put a mattress on the floor of the wagon,
at the back, and that's where my sister and I sat as we
rolled along; we slept whenever we wanted. When we
camped with relatives, often they would butcher a cow or
calf for us, then we'd stay with them until my mother got
all the meat cut up and dried.*

*"Nowadays we are following the white ways in most
everything we do. Take for example this thing that we are
sitting in (a travel-trailer). It got brought to this Sun
Dance camp fast, with a car. In my young days you
would have had to camp and sleep along the way, like
we always did with horses and wagons. Here in the camp
we would have put up our tipi, not slept in the wagon.*

*"Another thing is the telephone, which lets you know
everything right away. When there was a death in my
young days, someone had to go by horseback to notify
all the family and friends, and that took quite a bit of
time. Now we can just get on the phone and talk in all directions. Things like that make the life of today very, very
different.*

*"It's my thinking that the young people who live with all
these modern things have a very easy life. But they are
also poor because of it. This easy life seems to be very ex-
pensive. I see a lot of young families where the husband
and wife both work but they just barely make ends meet.
They have to pay for their homes, cars, lights, phone,
water, you name it. It seems that when young people get
paid they just hand over their money to pay the bills.
They won't be able to make much personal use of their
wages. That has changed from the way I knew it, as well.*

*"When those old people were still around we lived a sim-
ple life compared to now. We used wood for heat and
coal oil for light, and our horses for travelling around.
There weren't all these bills, and there weren't so many
things. Our life was much more simple and fun; that's
how I think of it now."*

Like my mom, Molly would prefer that life be simple life that
again, as it was in their young days, yet they both accept that it's
not going to happen, and that this is the will of the Creator.
That's a part of our tribal belief. They both have colour TV's
and phones at home, with good vehicles outside to drive them
around. They've managed to adapt their traditional faith to these
changes, but some things still surprise them each time they happen. As a ceremonial leader, Molly finds it especially hard at
times to watch as young people make changes to our customs
simply because they seem unwilling to learn the correct ways
from elders.

*"One of the hardest things for George and I is when
some young person wants to take part in our ceremonies
but instead of **asking** us how to do it, they just **tell** us
what they're going to do. We're not supposed to argue
about ceremonial things, so we just have to let them have
their way, but it sure is hard for us. It was never done
that way when we were young; we never told the old people what we were going to do; we always asked for their
directions."*

This is a problem those of us who are younger than Molly
have also experienced, that some people want to do things just
their own way, without finding out the proper traditions, or else
without knowing how to interpret those traditions correctly.
Sometimes they do this from ignorance, other times from stub-
bornness, and often it's just simply from a lack of proper knowledge. Molly is a singular kind of teacher in this day and age, but
her Montana division of our Blackfoot Confederacy has nearly

20,000 members so they can't all go and learn from her. But if not, where are they going to learn them from? A few young people are lucky enough to have a knowledgeable grandma or aunt or whatever, somewhere in their family, from whom they can get advice, but a great many don't.

"An example of change that I'm witnessing is this very Sun Dance gathering. In the past there would have been many old people camped here, especially for performing the important ceremonial functions. But here there are mostly young people, with just a couple of us who are old. It takes a long time to learn these ceremonies; the old people who ran them were patient and wise; it's hard to do that when you're young.

"My sister was adopted by an old Sun Dance woman, so in our family we all took her for a mother. An old warrior had given her the name First-to-Kill (same as Heavy Head's wife), and her husband was Wolf Plume. Together they put up Sun Dance lodges, and they also led the Sun Dance ceremonies for others, so I saw how they went about that kind of ceremonial work.

"First-to-Kill was a really kind and virtuous woman, but for some reason all her children died right away. One day she saw my mother big with my sister, so she said to her, 'Please let me have your child. It might bring me good luck!' My mother just told her, 'Yes, I will give it to you.' My mother had me after that, but First-to-Kill never did have any children of her own. She took my sister when she was just ten days old, then she and her old man raised her like their own. But we all kept in touch, and I often saw my sister. Eventually when that old couple died, they left my sister with all their land."

This is another custom that has changed among our people, that a mother would give up her child so readily to another woman, especially an elderly one. Molly might not notice that change as much as we who are younger, because as long as I've known her she's always had grandchildren, great-grandchildren and miscellaneous children around her household. I sometimes wonder if they will be among the last children to have such growing-up experiences around a wise elder? Will we who are younger still find time to let little kids hang around our homes when we get old, just for love and education? This is a part of our culture that cannot be learned in any other way.

> *"Through the years many old ladies painted my face and gave me their blessings. When I was young, whenever we went to a Sun Dance or other ceremony, my mother would bring my sister and me to one of the holy women to be painted. We just stayed by our mother most of the time, we didn't run around like the kids do nowadays. She explained things to us - old people often talked to their kids, and the kids would listen. It's very hard today to get kids to listen. Sometimes I was with another grandmother who was very respected for putting up Sun Dances. She would say, 'I had a bad dream, so I will paint you kids' faces to protect you from harm.' Those were her blessings. My mother gave her gifts of tobacco, or a dress, or even a pair of stockings, to show how she valued the blessings her children received."*

This face painting is a good example of our Blackfoot faith in prayers and nature. A qualified ceremonial person will mix a certain kind of red earth that we consider sacred, together with a bit of animal fat (from buffalo, in the past) and this will be rubbed on the face and wrists of the one seeking blessings, sometimes using certain designs, depending on the ceremony. Songs and other rituals often go with the blessing. In any case, there will be prayers for goodness on behalf of the one being painted. He or she will get strength from it, if they have faith. When this sacred painting is being done by your own grandmother, especially if you know that she also used to be painted by *her* grandmother, this heritage alone is enough to keep alive your faith. Women like Molly, and like my mom, were often given such face paintings while they were growing up. Those who are of my generation got them much more seldom, whereas nowadays there are many young people in our tribe who have never been painted at all. Letting kids like this know what it's all about, so they can at least make the choice if they want to, is another great challenge, since our customs don't let us go out after them like missionaries. We're supposed to wait until they come to us.

> *"The Medicine Pipe Bundle that George and I have was given to us through my mother and stepfather, Shoots First. My real father must have been involved with medicine pipes too, but I was never told anything about that. I was still young when he died and my mother remarried. At about that time my sister's first child, a boy named Lawrence, got that very dangerous sickness they call spinal meningitis. He was doctored all night by our medicine men, and they also brought him to the hospital, but nothing was helping. Finally the old folks made a vow to take over the Medicine Pipe bundle owned by Two Guns. It's very mystical, but right after that vow was made the boy got better.*
> *"My stepfather went and offered a smoke to Two Guns, asking him for his Medicine Pipe, and when Two Guns accepted they set the date for the transfer ceremony. My mother started making dried meat for the feast - they didn't have a lot of fancy food, like we serve nowadays - she just fed the people dried meat, boiled potatoes, fried bread and boiled eggs. A lot of old people were there and they went through the bundle transfer in the old time way."*

Molly is describing here the ritual by which all important Blackfoot medicine bundles are passed from one family to another. The keepers of most bundles, including Medicine Pipes, are a man and woman, usually a married couple but not necessarily so. With Medicine Pipe bundles there are also frequently one or two co-keepers, usually children of the main couple. All of them go through the lengthy transfer ritual together, which is led by an older couple who has had such a bundle, then learned the songs and other ritual knowledge. For this honor, the bundle recipients give many "payments" to the family giving up the bundle - horses, blankets, clothing, money and so forth, some of which goes to the ceremonial leaders and to other qualified people who are present. Usually the crowd at such a ceremony fills two large tipis, which for these occasions are fastened together. I might mention that the most recent Medicine Pipe bundle transfer I took part in happened to be led by George and Molly Kicking Woman, thus spanning quite an era.

> "My mother and stepfather must have had this Medicine Pipe bundle in their home for 15 years or so, when the old man died. My mother then fed it about three more times, that is, they had the ceremony for it, then something went wrong with her heart and she died. So my distant brother Dan Bull Plume took the bundle to his house and looked after it for a while. He even gave the feast and dance for it one time, though it wasn't actually transferred to him. He had a different one of his own.
> "Then one day he told us to go see him, my sister and I, to talk about the bundle. He wanted to have one of us take it. My sister didn't really want it in her home. She said right away, "You and George take it." Then she said, "My husband and I don't get along too well; we always separate." She was smart for making that decision; what she said was true, and it wouldn't have been good for the bundle.
> "George's mother was still alive then, so we went to her for advice. Don't forget that I was only about 23 and didn't really know what I should do.
> "As soon as she heard the full story she said, "If he told you to take it, then you might as well go ahead and take it.' That simple, and it was decided. That was in the 1940's and here over fifty years later and we still have it.
> "So, after the decision was made, we started sewing,

making quilts to help out with the transfer payments. We
had horses, and George's brother Medicine Bull contrib-
uted his wagon and harness. We gave a lot of things at
the transfer ceremony. At first Bull Plume said, 'I'll just
paint you for it. It belonged to your folks so you don't
have to go through the whole transfer, that way it won't
cost you so much." He knew we were young and didn't
have much. But my mother-in-law said, 'No, they will
have a proper transfer. Otherwise, people will talk; they
will say that my son and his wife are acting like full pipe
bundle owners, but they only got painted and paid just a
little bit.' So Bull Plume put us through the whole trans-
fer, which took two days. All kinds of rights were trans-
ferred to us."

When Molly says, "all kinds of rights were given to us," in
our culture and religion this is somewhat like being reborn. You
are a new person when you receive a medicine bundle, so you
are initiated to the various important things in life; eating, drinking, getting up, getting dressed, having a smoke, butchering, riding a horse, and so forth. All these initiations are part of our tribal faith; they help remind us of our spiritual obligations as
bundle keepers. This faith was continued right on through those
eras of strict missionary preaching, which is further evidence of
its tribal strength and power.

"George and I have had a good life with our medicine
pipe bundle. It's been in our home for a long time; we
raised all our children by it. The Creator is the main one
- you're only given so much time to live. Now I've lost
two of my children, my youngest son and my oldest
daughter, and I sure feel the loss. But it was the Crea-
tor's will, and I'm not offended. I can only keep praying
and taking care of my faith as I was taught to do."

Ceremonial leader Molly Kicking Woman is the last active link to a religious past that many younger Blackfeet are bringing back to life. For over a half century she and her husband George have been the keepers of an important Medicine Bundle that symbolizes the natural world of their tribal heritage. Having lived through a long time when all this was believed to be dying out, it has become Molly's greatest honour to give her traditional guidance and blessings to so many of the young.
Adolf Hungry Wolf Photo

12.

Maintaining the Faith on a Changing Path

It is a testimonial to the women of my mother's generation that they never lost faith in our tribal beliefs, even during those decades when everybody thought our tribal ways were finally dying out. Here is a strange fact: While women like my mother were young, most practitioners of our traditional beliefs were old; now that they themselves are old, most practitioners are comparatively young.

There was no way people like my mom could have imagined such a revival would take place. Books and articles frequently talked about "the vanishing race." The holders of our tribal medicine bundles were mostly old, and when they died the bundles were frequently sold to museums or private collectors. Within those bundles were the symbols of our traditional faith - feathers, skins and other objects, representing nature in our religious ceremonials. With each bundle that disappeared there was one less ceremony. Who could have guessed about today's "repatriation programs" that are bringing many of these bundles back from museums to again be part of our tribal circles.

This amazing revival got its main start with the so-called hippie movement of the 1960's, just as cultural participation in most tribes was reaching an all-time low. It was suddenly "cool" to be Indian, white kids from big cities all over said so, and tried to act like it, which affected some of us young Indians quite a bit. We figured that if it was alright for them to go around trying to be like Indians, then it was alright for us to be like ourselves too. This was like rebelling totally against what the boarding schools had forced upon us.

Some of us even started going to our grandfathers and grandmothers, the old time Indians that we'd been ashamed of, the ones we'd stayed away from. Now we wanted to know things from them, we wanted to learn something of our culture, our religion. And by golly, they weren't always that eager to teach us! Maybe they were suspicious at first of our motives, or else they were too used to being ignored themselves, even to being laughed at. It took patience and perseverance on our part, especially when we approached those who were really knowledgeable about sacred ceremonial ways.

We who were young knew little about the protocol that needs to be followed in approaching such elders for their knowledge and advice; there are many rules and etiquettes that must be treated respectfully and never fooled around with. I suppose the old people wanted to make sure we were sincere in our interests. That's where those of my mother's generation proved invaluable, helping us to bridge the generation gap. They sympathized with our eagerness to relearn something of our own heritage, yet they were also aware of the seriousness with which those old folks practiced and believed in their culture.

Respect is a major theme in those practices, especially respect for the Creator, and for all things of the Creation. There is a deep respect for nature and for the universe. Respect for other people too, especially children and elders. In their hearts, those of my mother's generation had so much respect for their elders that they never doubted the prayers and ceremonies practiced by them, even during the years when their minds were being confused by schools and churches.

"We loved and cherished our grandparents," recalls Margaret Hind Man, "so we knew that they could not be as evil as we were being told in school." Ceremonial leaders still regularly painted faces, and sometimes bestowed special blessings when the kids of my mom's generation were brought to medicine bundle openings. When my mom got older she sometimes helped cook the ceremonial feasts for bundle openings that were held by our relatives. More recently, for the past 25 years, she's been helping me and my own family with our bundle openings. That her only daughter participates so fully in traditional events brings back home the faith that she's kept alive since those young days with her grandparents.

While working on this part of my book it so happens that my mom and I camped together at one of the grandest of our religious celebrations, the one we call the Okan, or Medicine Lodge Ceremony, better known in English as the Sun Dance. There were three of these held this year alone, among the four divisions that make up our Blackfoot Confederacy. This particular one was the last of the three, the camp for it being among our Pikunni relatives, the Blackfeet Tribe of Montana, within sight of the Rocky Mountains and Glacier National Park.

A short explanation of the Sun Dance may be in order, for those of you not familiar with this ceremony, or at least with the Blackfoot version, which is quite a bit different from that of most other tribes who have Sun Dances (mainly those on the plains). For us, the main ritual goal of the Sun Dance is to build a large, round lodge of cottonwood posts that represents the home of the Sun, symbol of the Creator. A large, forked centre post in the middle of that round sun lodge represents the centre of the universe. Four days and nights of rituals are necessary before the raising of this centre pole, with a special woman and man representing all people of the tribe during those rituals. Any man may qualify for the position, though he should be of good character and this should become his lifelong commitment. However, only a pure and virtuous woman qualifies for her position, and it is she who wears the sacred crown of the ceremony, the so-called Natoas headdress, whose mystical origins are connected with the sun. Only she can take care of this headdress, and its "bundle" throughout the rest of the year. This is the highest honour that a woman can achieve in our tribal culture; those who do so are expected to serve as role models for everyone else.

Most of the Sun Dance women my mother has known were fairly old in age, especially those who were leaders of the complex ceremonies. In fact, during the years that I was growing up, the few remaining sun Dance women were all old ladies, and everyone assumed they would be the last of their kind. Thus, the camp to which my mom and I went had special significance, because a new Sun Dance woman was being initiated, a younger woman - more evidence of our cultural revival.

There were some difficulties and challenges at this particular Sun Dance, as there often are with our ceremonies; difficulties to be overcome by the holy man and woman, and also by the people in the camp. Some of the old people like to point out every mistake made by those of us who are younger. Then there are other old people who tell us not to pay these critics any mind. Having so few elders left who know much about ceremonial things makes the challenges even more complicated, especially since some of those who know very little insist that they know a lot, while many of the young aren't sure who knows what.

The required vow to "put up" a Sun Dance was in this case made by an unmarried young man, a fairly common custom back in the warpath days, when such young men made vows in times of great danger to help them get through. In this case it took some time for the young man to locate an eligible woman partner, then even longer to find an available Natoas headdress bundle that she could use.

Although there are now somewhere around a dozen Sun Dance women in our tribe, and about the same number of men, only two or three of them know the complicated ceremony well enough to lead it, although they all join in to help, especially with the songs and prayers that go on continually.

When I look at our culture on a broad scope it seems that it has always undergone changes, additions, and variations. It is said that a culture and religion will stagnate if there are no changes. The Blackfoot ways are so complex that they couldn't possibly have developed overnight, so they must have come about through additions and changes. The important thing is that we maintain the faith of our ancestors, their faith in the powers of nature. The Creator put us on this earth for a reason, and we get satisfaction from giving thanks to the Creator for that.

Not long ago my daughter and I visited an old Sun Dance woman and listened to her thoughts about our culture and its changes. She's kind of shy, so I won't mention her name, but what she said speaks for an important segment of our tribe's older people. Here's what she told us.

"When I was young and sick, I had a dream about the Sun lodge. It was a strong dream, so I told it to my old people and they discussed it for a long time. Most said the dream meant that I should put up a Sun Dance, but my grandmother argued hard against it. She knew how severe it would be for me.

"I will just tell you that I finally went ahead, and that for those four days and nights when I fasted, the old people were so strict with me that I could not even move on my own. When someone came to the tipi door I could not look up. If my hair fell in my face I could not brush it aside.

"I just had to sit holy and be quiet. On the last night, after they sang for us, they made me lay my head down on a pillow of juniper. The needles were very sharp, but what bothered me most was that I have a great fear of spiders and I kept thinking one of them would crawl out of that juniper and into my ears.

"It's a hard, straight life you have to follow as a Sun Dance woman. You cannot talk mean about people. You cannot talk bad to them. You always have to be kind to everyone."

This last part was especially stressed by the other old Sun Dance women I've known. They were at every Sun Dance ceremony that took place while they were still alive. Unfortunately, they've been gone for years, whereas the elder speaking here doesn't like to attend them anymore, because she thinks the people are making too many changes. From her strict point of view she is probably right, but for my family and many others, the spiritual benefits we get from each Sun Dance are still very wonderful. I guess it's human nature to complain, but many of us are grateful that our tribal Sun Dance remains alive and continues helping our tribe members renew their faith in life.